Copyright

CH01472165

All

The characters and e͏   ͏.͏.͏.͏.͏.͏.͏.͏.͏.͏ in this book are
fictitious. Any similarity to real persons, living or dead, is
coincidental and not intended by the author.

No part of this book may be reproduced, or stored in a
retrieval system, or transmitted in any form or by any
means, electronic, mechanical, photocopying, recording,
or otherwise, without express written permission of the
publisher.

ISBN: 9798306916507

Cover design by: Erelis Design
Library of Congress Control Number: 2018675309
Printed in the United States of America

HAWK FOOTBALL CLUB

By Stevie Suarez

CHAPTER ONE

LIAM

Liam McKeever received the ball on the half-turn and spun around a big defender. He slid a pass through to his best friend, Ronan O'Kelly, who played striker. Liam and Ronan had played for Park Celtic since they were five years old. Ronan used his electric speed to beat the last defender, took the ball around the keeper and slotted his finish into the bottom corner. The goal net bulged as the keeper dived a split second too late and Ronan wheeled away, pumping his fist into the air. Liam followed Ronan towards the corner flag, and the two friends dropped to their knees and slid across the grass.

"What a goal!" Liam exclaimed as their knee-slide came to a stop. They laughed as the rest of the team sprinted to join the celebration, every boy cheering and clapping with joy.

"Great pass. Unbelievable assist," Ronan replied, barely getting the words out before Paddy, Jim, and the entire Park Celtic team fell on top of them.

It was the last game of the season, and if Park Celtic won, they would be league champions. Liam got to his feet and jogged back to the centre circle, waving to his mum, dad, and younger sister Penny, who watched from the sidelines. A bright sun shone in a clear blue sky. The pitch was dry and fast, perfect conditions for the last game of the Kildare under-twelve Premier League season. The opposition trudged into their positions for kick-off, their heads down and hands on their hips. It was two–one to Park Celtic, and Liam guessed there were about ten minutes left to play.

The referee blew his whistle and pointed to the ball to indicate that Crannock Villa could kick-off.

"We need another one," panted Ronan, winking at Liam from across the centre circle. "But these lads look like they're finished already."

Liam shook his head at Ronan's banter, and the Crannock Villa forward, a tall lad with curly hair, rewarded Ronan with a furious scowl. Ronan was small for his age, but he was fast. Lightning fast. As a central midfielder, Liam loved nothing more than sending Ronan away with a threaded-through ball, and they had scored more goals through that combination than Liam could remember.

The Crannock Villa forward passed the ball back to his midfielder, and the game was back on. The opposition passed it around neatly, using triangles to work the ball to the left-back and into their winger. Play moved fast, and Liam and his team fought hard to win the midfield battle. Liam tackled a quick midfielder and won a header against the tall striker. The final ten minutes seemed to last a lifetime, and Liam was sucking in huge breaths and leaning on his knees as Crannock Villa prepared to take a corner.

"Keep it tight, boys," warned Paddy. "Liam, mark the big lad!"

Liam wasn't the tallest on the team, but he wasn't the smallest either, and he always fancied himself to win headers from corners. The Crannock Villa player took the corner, sweeping it in with his right foot. The ball soared high above the players who jostled each other inside the six-yard box. Liam lost the flight of it for a moment as the sun blinded him. His stomach churned with fear as he thought an opposition player might score to level the match. His vision cleared and Liam spotted the ball coming in his direction. The tall striker shoved Liam with his shoulder and Liam barged him out of the way. He jumped, rising above the striker, and headed the ball away.

"Let's go, Liam!" Paddy called, but Liam had landed and was already sprinting away from the box. Ronan had picked up the ball. He beat a Crannock Villa midfielder with a step-over and set off running up the wing. Liam ran straight through the middle of the pitch, racing past two Villa defenders as he tried to keep up with Ronan. His best friend glanced at him and crossed the ball with his left foot. The ball swerved towards the goal, just ahead of Liam's run. So, Liam did the only thing he could do. He dived, meeting the ball with his forehead and sent it crashing into the back of the net.

The crowd of watching parents went wild. Liam's teammates crashed into him, ruffling his hair and patting him on the back. He smiled from ear to ear. A diving header! What a way to win the match! The referee blew the whistle, and it was all over. Park Celtic had won the league, and the team laughed and sang together to celebrate.

"What a game!" Liam whooped as he plonked down next to Penny in the back seat of Dad's car after the game.

"Well done, son," smiled Dad, turning from the front seat to bump Liam's fist with his own. "We're all so proud of you!"

"I love my team! Mum, did you see my goal?" Liam asked eagerly. Mum didn't turn around from the passenger seat. "Mum, did you hear me? Did you see my goal?"

Mum slowly turned around to face Liam, and he noticed with surprise that she wasn't smiling like Dad. "It was brilliant," she said, but her voice sounded quiet and sad. She paused, glanced at Dad, and then turned back to Liam and Penny. "Enjoy the feeling, Liam. I hate to tell you this now, but that could have been your last game for Park Celtic."

CHAPTER TWO

LIAM

Two weeks after winning the league, Liam stared out of a small, round window watching a rolling, grey sea. Waves crashed against the sides of the car ferry and if he squinted, Liam could just about see the shadow of Ireland's coastline disappearing into the distance. He had boarded the ferry at Dublin Port, heading towards Holyhead in North Wales.

"How long does it take to drive from Holyhead to Freyton?" asked Liam's little sister Penny.

"About an hour and a half," answered Mum.

"Will my new school be like my old school?"

"Yes, but with lots of new friends to make."

"It won't be like our old school," sighed Liam. He turned away from the window and slumped in the chair, arms folded across his chest. The family sat on hard chairs around a narrow table. "All my friends are in Ireland. My team is in Ireland. What do I want to go to England for?"

"We've talked about this, buddy," Dad said softly. "My job has moved to England, and we must move with it. You'll like England. Freyton is slap bang in between Liverpool and Manchester. I'll be able to take you to Anfield to see the Reds play. That's something, right?"

Liam shrugged. "Yeah, I suppose so." Liam loved Liverpool Football Club, and Dad brought him over from Ireland once every season to watch them play. He had been four times so far, and seeing his heroes play in real life was amazing. "But what about school? What about Park Celtic?"

"Come on." Dad stood and held his hand out to Liam. "Let's go out on the top deck and look at the sea."

Liam took Dad's hand and rose from his seat. The ferry had left at 7.30am, so Mum and Dad bought breakfast for Liam and Penny once they had parked the car on a lower deck and climbed three flights of stairs to the passenger deck. The ferry was huge. It had a cinema, slot machines, a kids' play area, a bar, and even cabins where people could sleep if they wished. Liam followed Dad out of the ferry's restaurant towards the stairwell. He staggered as the ship lurched, and took three steps to his right and then to his left. The sea heaved beneath them as if it tried to push the ferry back to Ireland. Liam wished it would.

Dad climbed the stairs and opened a heavy door to the outer deck. He held the door open, and Liam ducked under his arm and out into an ice-cold wind, whipping his hair from his face. Dad let go of the door, and it slammed shut to leave them both leaning into a wind so strong that, for a moment, Liam thought it might lift him off his feet. Dad put his arm around Liam's shoulder and helped him walk to the iron rail so they could look out at the endless, heaving waves.

"I know it's hard for you, son," said Dad. "But once you settle into school in England, you will make new friends."

"I don't want to make new friends," choked Liam, thinking of Ronan and the school football matches they played every lunchtime against the boys in the year above them. Great matches full of goals, penalties, tackles, fouls and wild celebrations.

"England is a big place. There are more people in Manchester than there are in the whole of Ireland, and lots of people there love football. You can join a new team in Freyton."

"I don't want to join a new team, Dad. I play for Park Celtic." Liam swallowed a lump in his throat and tried to stop himself from crying. Playing football was everything to him. He went to sleep thinking about it, and it was the first thing on his mind when he woke up. He loved training, playing matches, kicking around at school, and even playing on the green outside his house with Ronan and the other lads who lived close by.

"It's going to be fine, Liam. Lots of people move jobs and change where they live. In six months' time, you'll love England just as much as you did living in Ireland."

Dad pulled Liam into a hug, and he wrapped his arms around his father's waist. His tears soaked into Dad's coat and Liam wondered if his friends would miss him, how Park Celtic would do when the league kicked off, and if he would ever play football again.

CHAPTER THREE

TOM

Tom jogged on the spot, eagerly waiting for Hawk Football Club's pre-season friendly to kick-off. He played right-back, next to his friend Jake, who played centre-back. The right-winger Leo stared at the sky ahead of them, picking his nose.

"It's going to be a long season," sighed Jake, shaking his head as he watched Leo.

"Is this lot any good?" asked Tom.

Jake shrugged. "Coach said they came bottom of their league last season. So, let's hope not."

Hawk FC finished at the bottom of their Freyton Town league last season. They hadn't won one match. Their star striker, Sergio, was late, meaning Hawk started this friendly with only ten men. Things didn't look promising for the new season.

The ref blew his whistle, and the match kicked off. The opposition, a team from Liverpool with a red and white striped kit, kicked the ball around their back four. Their left-back took possession and fizzed a quick through ball down the line. It flew past Leo whilst he still had a finger so far up his nose, that Tom thought he might scratch his brain. Tom ran forward to intercept the pass Leo hadn't even seen. Just as Tom was about to reach the ball, a super-rapid winger from the other team came out of nowhere and took it around Tom as if he were a statue. He turned just in time to see the winger drill a shot into the bottom corner of the goal. The keeper dived, or at least attempted to dive, and was so slow that the ball was in the back of the net before he hit the ground like a sack of potatoes. Mark was the goalkeeper, and to say he was slow was like saying a snail was not quite ready to run in the Olympic Games.

The opposition winger wheeled away and ran past Tom with a finger pressed to his lips. He was actually shushing Tom, and the match had only just begun!

"You were right, mate," gulped Tom, turning to Jake. "It is going to be a long season."

Just as the match was about to kick-off again, Sergio came sprinting across the field with his boots in his hand. Billy, the Hawk FC coach, helped him quickly tie his boots and pull on the number ten jersey. Tom breathed a sigh of relief.

"Let's go, Sergio!" Tom called, waving to his friend. Sergio was the team's best player, perhaps their only decent player. If they stood any chance of winning a match this season, then Sergio was the boy to save them.

Sergio jogged to the centre circle and took the kick-off. He passed it all the way back to Jake, spun off a midfielder and charged towards the goal. Jake put his foot through the ball, launching it high towards the box. The ball came down like a swooping eagle and Sergio took it on his chest. Tom held his breath. Everything around him went quiet, and it was as if time slowed. The ball cushioned against Sergio's chest. He turned at the hip and shaped up to volley the ball like prime Zinedine Zidane. But then a figure in red and white stripes crashed into him like a train and Sergio crumpled into a mess on the turf.

"What was that?" Coach Billy yelled from the sideline.

"Ah, ref!" Jake yelled, hands in the air.

Tom's heart sank. Sergio was down and had only been on the pitch for thirty seconds! The ref waved Billy on, and he jogged to where Sergio rolled on the ground, clutching his ankle. Billy lifted Sergio up and helped him to limp off the pitch. After that, the team from Liverpool ran rings around Hawk FC.

Tom did his best, getting in a few slide tackles and winning a header from a corner. Tom, Jake, and the lads finished the game barely able to stand up, their legs aching and their hair dripping with sweat.

"That's ten–nil, lad," bragged the winger who had shushed Tom earlier in the game. "You lot are rubbish!"

The opposition left the pitch laughing and shaking their heads, while Tom and the Hawk FC players hung their heads in shame.

"We did well," Coach Billy comforted them as he collected the jerseys after the game. "You tried your best. That's the most important thing."

"Trying is fine," said Tom, "but winning is better."

"Winning isn't everything."

"Thanks, Billy." Tom handed him the jersey, which Billy washed and folded every week so that the team could play every match looking their best, even though their kit was old, faded, and ragged.

"We can't go the entire season without a win again," moaned Jake as he and Tom trudged towards their bikes.

"We need a miracle," Tom replied.

CHAPTER FOUR

LIAM

Liam's new school was a five-minute walk from his house. He left the front door of the McKeever family's new home, turned to wave at Mum, and set off for his first day. It was a sunny morning, and his new navy blue jumper chafed his neck beneath the straps of his backpack. It was bad enough that this was his first day at high school, but he had to go without knowing even one person. Ronan and the boys back home in Ireland were all about to start high school together, and here was Liam, walking out into the unknown without one single friendly face waiting for him.

Mum had bought Liam two pairs of grey trousers, which felt three sizes too big, the navy blue jumper, which itched his skin like nettle stings, and an ugly school tie that Dad had tied over breakfast. Worst of all was the blazer. A navy blue suit jacket with the Elm Tree Comprehensive badge sewn into the left side stood proudly upon Liam's chest. Liam walked alongside the red-bricked houses of his street, turned left, passed the shop, and crossed the road at a zebra crossing. He turned a corner and merged with a crowd of kids, all walking towards a sprawling building made of steel-grey concrete. The sound of children talking, laughing and shouting rose above the crowd like the noise inside a football stadium.

A shiver ran across Liam's shoulders at the sheer number of kids around him. His school in Ireland had only one class in each year, and there had been just seven other boys in Liam's class. Three older boys barged past him, laughing as he stumbled and almost dropped his bag. Two girls pointed at him and giggled and Liam couldn't help his face turning red. A pang of fear turned his stomach over, and Liam wished Dad's job hadn't moved to England. It was unbearable. Too big, too many people, accents he couldn't understand. And he was all alone.

Liam reached the school gates and entered a winding maze of corridors in search of his form room, the room where he must report to each morning before going off to his different classes. The school smelled like a hospital and around every corner, Liam found more kids laughing and pointing in his direction. He couldn't understand it at first, but then it hit him. He was the only person in the entire school wearing a blazer. Every other kid just had the jumper, tie and shirt.

"Who do you think you are?" drawled a sneering voice. Liam turned to find a tall boy with red hair and freckles staring down at him.

"He looks like a little lord," sniggered one of six boys gathered about the towering redhead.

"Like a prince," jeered another. "Or a princess." They all laughed, and Liam wished he were a tortoise so he could shrink and hide in his shell.

"Why are you wearing that?" demanded the redhead. "Do you think you're better than us or something?"

"No," Liam stuttered. "My mum got it for me. I didn't know..."

"Your mummy?" scoffed one boy, a stocky lad with a buzz cut. "What a loser."

They grabbed at Liam's blazer and spun him around. Everybody in the corridor hooted with laughter and Liam struggled to hold back tears. He pushed the boys away from him and, by accident, his finger poked into the tall boy's eye. The boy screeched in pain and pushed Liam so hard that he dropped his bag.

"You there!" shouted a woman's voice from along the corridor. "Leave that boy alone!" A cross-looking teacher with glasses wagged a finger at the boys and they let Liam go.

"Leave him, Jax," said Buzz Cut. "He's not worth

it."

"Watch out, muppet," growled Jax, the red-haired boy. "I'll get you."

They hurried away, laughing, and Liam shrank against the wall. He took off his blazer, hastily shoved it in his bag, and wondered if his life could get any worse.

CHAPTER FIVE

TOM

Tom cycled from his house to the Hawk's Nest, the nickname everybody used for the Hawk FC playing fields.

"Our first day at high school wasn't so bad, was it?" asked Jake as Tom rested his bike against the clubhouse wall.

"Yeah, it was all right. I can't wait for the school football trials, though," said Tom.

"Do you think the school will have a team?"

"Definitely. You'd make the squad no problem."

"We'll play for a good team for a change."

"We can't finish bottom of the league again this season. There's relegation this year for the first time."

"So, if we finish bottom this year, we go down?"

"Yeah. Hawk FC down in the second division. We'd only get to play once every few weeks. All our best players would leave. What a nightmare!"

"Would you stay if we went down?"

Tom raised his eyebrows in surprise. "I'd never leave the Hawks! But if we lost you and Sergio, we might even finish bottom of the second division, never mind the Freyton Premier League."

"Oh no. Look!" Jake pointed to the car park where Sergio stepped slowly out of his dad's car. Sergio grabbed a set of crutches and limped over to where Tom and Jake waited by the clubhouse.

"What happened?" asked Tom in dismay.

"I've done my ankle," said Sergio, frowning. "That tackle in the friendly was a bad one. I had to go to the hospital, and they gave me these crutches."

"How long are you going to be out?"

"A few months at least."

"It's going to be a long season, boys," sighed Jake, and the three teammates shook their heads.

The clubhouse door swung open, and Coach Billy came striding out with a bag of footballs slung across one shoulder, and a stack of training cones in one hand. That door, once black, was now a faded grey colour covered with names and pictures scratched into the wood by teenagers who hung around the training fields at night. The clubhouse itself was a one-storey building with pale white cladding, and walls daubed in bright graffiti. Scrawled pictures and words in red, blue, yellow and green had covered the walls for as long as Tom could remember. Inside were home and away dressing rooms with rickety wooden benches, leaking roofs, and a toilet that always stank so badly that Tom had to hold his breath whenever he went in. There was a dressing room for the referees and a kit room with spare kits, balls, training cones, corner flags, goal nets, and all the other bits and pieces that made Hawk FC a football team.

"Right lads," announced Coach Billy, a broad smile splitting his chubby face, "let's get going. Only a couple of weeks until the season starts."

He strode towards the playing fields, where the rest of the squad waited for him. Tom and Jake followed, while Sergio sat to watch beside the clubhouse. Coach Billy laid out the cones the same way he always did and sent the team off to run laps around the pitch.

"Looks like passing drills again," muttered Jake as he and Tom ran side by side.

"We do the same thing every week," replied Tom. "Look at John. He hasn't been able to run a lap since we were seven years old."

"He tries, though, Tom." Jake turned and waved to John, who ran twenty paces behind the rest of the team. Rosy-cheeked, his kit was tight about his tummy and legs, and sweat plastered his hair to his head. "That's what Hawk is about, right? It isn't about winning or losing. It's about us. The lads, playing together, sticking up for each other."

"You're right, Jake. Same as usual." Tom smiled, punched Jake on the shoulder, and broke out into an all-out sprint. "Last one to finish smells like a Darkstone Rangers player!"

Jake set off after him as Tom raced around the pitch. The two boys laughed together, and the rest of the team joined in. The lads collapsed together as they reached Coach Billy and his neat lines of cones, rolling around, laughing about the race. Tom sat up and glanced around at the tatty clubhouse, the sloped pitch and the rusty goalposts. He smiled at Coach Billy. The old man was always excited to run training, even though they had done the same session every week for years. Jake was right. This was Hawk FC. It was about friends, football, and fun, and Tom loved it.

CHAPTER SIX

LIAM

Liam lay on his bed, staring up at the bedroom ceiling. His phone lay on the bed beside him, but Liam couldn't look at it. Ronan had sent a photo of all the Park Celtic team starting school together. They all looked so happy. Every time Liam thought about home, it brought a painful lump to his throat. He should be there with them, in classes with his friends, starting pre-season with Park Celtic as league champions. Instead, he was in England, alone, with people who laughed at him, and at a huge school where he didn't know anybody.

Liam's bedroom opened, and Mum poked her head through the gap.

"I'm sorry your first day didn't go well," she said. She pushed the door fully open and sat on the edge of Liam's bed, placing a loving hand on his leg.

"It was horrible, Mum," said Liam quietly. "Everybody picked on me because of that stupid blazer. I don't want to go back there tomorrow. I just want to go home."

"We live here now Liam. This is our home. You will make friends, and things will get better."

"Why do we have to live here? Can't we just go home?"

"Dad's job is here now. We've been through this a hundred times. It feels hard now, but you will get used to it."

"Can't Dad just get a job back at home in Ireland?" Liam knew the answer and had asked a dozen times already. Mum just shook her head.

"Your sister had a lovely time at her new school today."

"It's not the same, Mum. Penny's in primary school. I'm with the big kids. Have you seen the size of my school? I don't even get to play football anymore. I hate it here."

"Please don't say that, Liam. We must do our best to fit in here in Freyton. I have some amazing news for you, though."

Liam sat up eagerly. "A trip home to Ireland?"

"No, I'm afraid not. But I have found you a new football team to join. A local team."

"Really?" Liam smiled for the first time since leaving Ireland. "Do you think they'll let me join?"

"You're an excellent player, Liam. Any team would love to have you."

"What's the team called?"

"The Darkstone Rangers. I emailed their coach, and he replied. They have training this evening, and you can join them."

Liam leapt across the bed and wrapped his arms around her. "Thanks, Mum."

Two hours later, Liam sat in the back of Mum's car with his grip socks on, cut socks over them and shin pads tucked inside. He wore a pair of black shorts and a plain blue football training t-shirt. His stomach felt empty even though he'd eaten a gigantic piece of lasagne for dinner. Nerves, Liam thought. He had only ever played for Park Celtic, where he knew all the players and coaches and they knew him. Liam would have to prove himself at a new club. He would need to show them what he could do and try to find a position to play in every week. He was happy, though, despite the nerves. Joining a new team would at least give him some teammates and a way to make friends in his new home.

Mum turned the car into a lane twenty minutes from home and the first thing Liam saw was an enormous sign with *Darkstone Rangers* in bright lettering and a picture of a barking bulldog. The sign was black and white, and whilst it was a little foreboding, it also made Liam's heart beat faster with excitement. The tiny stones of the car park crunched beneath the car tyres and Liam gaped at three lush green pitches, an astro-turf pitch that looked brand new, and a clubhouse three times the size of Park Celtic's.

"Wow," marvelled Mum. "This place looks really professional."

Liam stepped out of the car and walked nervously to where a coach dressed in black waited outside the clubhouse. The coach was tall and broad-shouldered, with dark eyes and a long face framed by a jet-black beard.

"Liam?" barked the coach, his voice as full of gravel as the car park.

"Yes, this is Liam," replied Mum with a smile.

"Your mummy can't speak for you if you are going to be a Darkstone player, lad." The coach frowned down at Liam, and Mum crossed her arms. Her face was like thunder at the coach's rudeness.

"Erm, yes, I'm Liam," Liam faltered, his voice coming out much quieter than he wanted.

The clubhouse door burst open at that moment, and fifteen players bustled out. They wore all-black training kits and were tall and muscular. Their boots clattered on the stone pathway leading to the pitches, and Liam felt tiny as he stood next to them.

"Quiet!" the coach bellowed, and every single player hushed. "Attention!" The players hurried into a straight line, chins high, chests puffed out and arms straight down at their sides like they were in the army. "This is Liam, a new lad who will train with us this evening. Let's see what he's made of. Show him what it means to be a Darkstone Rangers player."

Liam stared along the line of Darkstone footballers, and then his breath caught in his throat as he recognised the tallest of them. A red-haired boy who sneered down at him.

"Do you know this boy, Jax?" demanded the coach, noticing the look of recognition between them.

"Yes, sir," said Jax. "He started at our school. Irish lad. Bit of a muppet, sir."

Liam took two involuntary steps back, wanting to be anywhere but there. As he looked along the line, Liam recognised Jax's friend Buzz Cut, standing with the other boys who had laughed at him in school.

"Really?" said the coach.

"He poked me in the eye, sir. Fancies himself as a bit of a hard man, sir."

"Well. We know how to deal with bullies here, don't we, lads?" The coach scowled at Liam.

"Yes, sir!" the entire team shouted at once. "Crush them, hurt them, beat them, own them!" Every player roared the words together, eyes glaring at Liam, and the force of it hit him like a hammer blow.

"I don't know what kind of team you are running here," said Mum, grabbing Liam by the hand, "but we want no part of it." She pulled Liam away, and he turned, almost running back to the car.

"Mummy's boy!" Jax called after him.

"You are weak," the coach growled. "There is no room for weaklings at the Darkstone Rangers."

Liam reached the car and dove into the back seat. As Mum drove away, he saw the Darkstone Rangers players pointing and laughing at him. Things just kept getting worse. Even the football team in Freyton was horrible. He picked up his phone and saw a message from Ronan and the lads back home. It was a selfie of them all on the first night of pre-season training. They all looked so happy, and Liam couldn't stop the tears from rolling down his face.

CHAPTER SEVEN

TOM

Tom brought his ball to school on the second day of term. It was a Premier League ball with barely a scuff on its bright orange and blue pictures. He and Jake took turns doing keep-ups, juggling the football all the way down the long road to school. Jake misplaced a kick with his left foot just before the school gates. The ball bounced away towards a boy standing behind the gates, almost hidden in the shadows.

The boy flicked the ball up with his right foot, juggled it twice with his left, bounced the ball on each knee and then headed it back to Jake.

"Not bad, mate," said Tom, appreciating the skill. "You almost did a Maradona seven there."

"Maradona seven?" said the boy in an unfamiliar

accent. He was taller than Tom, with brown hair.

"Yeah, you know, like Maradona, the old Argentinian player? You have to keep it up with the left foot, right foot, each knee, each shoulder and then a header."

"I'll give that a try." The boy smiled sadly.

Tom and Jake carried on beyond the gates and towards the school building.

"I've never seen him before," said Jake. "He mustn't play for a team in Freyton."

"I didn't recognise him either," Tom replied. "He looked decent with the ball, though."

Tom and Jake entered the school, waved to John and Leo from the team, and went to their first class, which was maths. Despite being in the same classroom, the alphabetical desk arrangement put Jake on the opposite side of the room to Tom. When the bell went to signify the end of the lesson, Tom had spent half of it trying to understand the mysteries of long division and the other half looking out of the window, wondering if Liverpool would beat Manchester City at the weekend.

Tom's chair squeaked on the classroom floor as he shot to his feet, stuffed his pencil case and books in his backpack, and headed for the door.

"You were almost asleep in there," teased Jake in the corridor. They walked amongst the press of kids, all heading towards their next class.

"I was wide awake!" exclaimed Tom. "I saw you with your finger in your ear."

"I did not have my finger in my ear!"

"You did, mate. You pulled out a massive ear bogey!"

Jake saw the smirk on Tom's face, and they laughed. They turned a corner toward their English classroom and stopped suddenly. A group of boys blocked the corridor, shouting and cheering.

"What's going on here?" asked Jake.

"It's that lot from Darkstone Rangers," realised Tom. "I recognise the big lad, Jax."

"They win the league every year. Not shy in gloating about it either."

"Remember when they beat us seven–nil in the cup two years ago?"

"Of course I remember. Wait a minute! They've got someone trapped there!"

Tom stepped to the side and saw that Jake was right. The Darkstone players had made a circle around a boy and were pushing him around and laughing at the frightened look on his face. "It's the boy from this morning who did the keep-ups by the gate."

"You're right. Why are they doing that to him?"

Jax ripped the boy's bag from his back, unzipped it, and emptied the contents all over the floor, much to the amusement of the rest of the Darkstone players.

"We've got to do something," said Tom. He was already moving towards the group and Jake followed. He grabbed the bag from Jax's hand and reached for the frightened boy.

"Leave him alone," shouted Jake. He and Tom pulled the terrified boy towards them. The Darkstone players roared angrily and turned on Tom and Jake.

"It's those idiots from Hawk FC," said Jax with a sneer. "This is none of your business, losers!"

For a horrific moment, Tom thought the Darkstone players would attack him until they paused, distracted by something over Tom's shoulder.

"Back off, Darkstone," came a furious voice.

Tom turned and sighed with relief to see six Hawk lads standing behind him. Big Dave shouldered his way through them to stand between Tom and Jax. Dave played centre-back for Hawk alongside Jake. Dave was from a tough family, well known throughout Freyton. His brother had been expelled from school, and some people said his dad was a gangster. But Dave was one of the nicest lads on the team, and certainly the toughest.

"All right, Dave," said Jax, holding up his hands to say he didn't want any trouble. "We were just joking around."

The Darkstone team backed away and Tom turned to the scared boy.

"Don't worry about them," Tom said gently. "They're bullies. Their team is all horrible."

"Thanks," stammered the boy, unable to take his eyes off the floor.

"Lads, help him pick up his stuff," ordered Jake, and the Hawk lads all got down on their knees and picked up everything Jax had emptied from the boy's bag. Big Dave passed the bag to the boy, who took it with an unhappy smile.

"What's your name?" asked Tom.

"Liam," whispered the boy.

"I'm Tom, and this is Jake, Dave, Leo, John, Mark and Adam. You aren't from around here, are you?"

"I've just moved to Freyton from Ireland."

"We saw your keep-ups this morning. Do you play football?"

"I did when I lived back home, yeah."

"We all play for a local team. Hawk FC. You should come down and train with us. You might like it."

"Are you sure you want to inflict that on the lad,

Tom?" joked Leo, and the rest chuckled.

"We aren't that good, but we have a laugh, and we do our best," added Dave.

"We're training tomorrow. At the Hawk's Nest fields. Fancy trying it?" asked Tom.

"I'd love to. Thanks again for helping me."

Dave put his arm around Liam's shoulders and the Hawk FC boys walked Liam to his next class. He seemed happier already, and based on his ball juggling, Tom was hopeful that Liam would make a fantastic addition to their team.

CHAPTER EIGHT

LIAM

Liam waited in Mum's car outside the Hawk FC clubhouse. He wore his football boots, shin pads, a plain pair of socks, shorts and a t-shirt. He had a full set of Park Celtic training gear at home, but didn't want to wear his old gear to his first training session with a new team.

"Are you sure this is the right place?" Mum wondered, staring at the graffiti-daubed clubhouse and the shabby-looking facilities.

"This is it, Mum," said Liam. "It doesn't look like much. But the boys were really nice to me. I just want to give it a go."

"Well, it can't be much worse than that awful Darkstone place, I suppose."

"I'll be grand, Mum." As Liam opened the car door,

Tom, the boy who had first helped Liam in the corridor, arrived at the clubhouse on his bike.

"Enjoy yourself." Mum beamed at him, and Liam smiled back.

Liam closed the car door and walked slowly to where Tom was locking his bike. When Tom heard his footsteps, he turned.

"You came, then?" Tom grinned.

"Yes. Is it still OK for me to train?" asked Liam.

"Of course it is. Nice boots!"

"Thanks. What kind of stuff do you work on in training?"

"The same stuff every week. You'll see. What position do you play?"

"Centre-midfield normally, but I would play anywhere."

"Evening, lads," said a grey-haired man with a round belly and cheerful face.

"Coach Billy, this is Liam," announced Tom. "Is it all right if he trains with us and joins the team?"

"Yes, of course it is. Welcome along, lad," said Billy, warmly. He stretched out a large hand and ruffled Liam's hair.

"Thanks, coach," said Liam. He couldn't help but smile at how welcome he felt at Hawk FC compared to the serious army-like Darkstone Rangers.

The rest of the team arrived on their bikes or walking across the fields, and every boy who arrived said hello to Liam. Some even offered him their hands for a fist-bump, which he returned happily. Training began with two laps jogging around the pitch. The players laughed and joked as they went. Most of the lads supported either Liverpool or Manchester United, and there was a lot of banter about how well or how badly each team was doing in the league. Liam supported Liverpool and so laughed at all the jokes about the Manchester United players.

"Everybody in!" Coach Billy said after the laps. He led them in some basic stretching drills, and Liam stretched his hamstrings, calves, and groin. "Let's get the passing drill going." As soon as Billy uttered those words, the entire team groaned.

"Why is everyone moaning?" asked Liam, confused.

"You'll find out in about four weeks' time," said Tom. "Trust me."

Coach Billy had set up the training cones in two rows, and each player took up a position on a red or black cone. Billy blew his whistle, and the team passed balls with their right foot and left foot across the space. Liam took up a place opposite a boy called Leo and they exchanged passes.

"Well done, Liam," Coach Billy praised, as Liam controlled the ball with his left foot and passed it with his right.

Once the passing was over, Coach Billy set the cones up for a rondo drill. Liam knew what to do from training back in Ireland. In a rondo, one player stands in the middle of a tight circle of other players. The other players must pass the ball around quickly and the player in the middle must try to intercept and win the ball. Liam went in the middle first and held a green bib in his hand to identify him as the middle player. The players fizzed quick passes, but then one took a heavy touch, and Liam darted in and won the ball. After that, he made sure his passes were crisp, and he was not in the middle again for the rest of the rondo.

"One v' ones now, guys," announced Coach Billy, and blew his whistle to show that the rondo was over. He sent half of the group to the halfway line and the other half to line up behind the goal. Liam went with the players on the halfway line. He loved one versus one attacking and defending drills. Attacking was one of Liam's strong points. At least, he hoped it was. He had never played in England before, and England was ten times the size of Ireland. It was the home of the Premier League, of Liverpool, Manchester United, Manchester City, Chelsea, and Arsenal.

Coach Billy blew his whistle and the drill began.

Liam kicked the ball to the first defender, Adam, who took a heavy touch and passed the ball back to Liam. It was Liam's job now to beat Adam and try to score a goal. Liam started running, keeping the ball close to him as he picked up speed. Adam ran at him and rushed into a challenge, so Liam jinked the ball around him and smashed it in the bottom corner.

"What a goal!" called a player behind him. Liam turned to see Big Dave, an absolute giant of a boy, giving him a thumbs-up. Liam smiled and returned the gesture. He went to the back of the line and watched the rest of the team progress through the drill. Most of the players were slow, didn't know how to defend and couldn't use both feet on the ball, but they had fun. The training pitch was full of laughter and encouragement. The Hawks cheered every tackle and goal, and though they weren't anywhere near as talented as Park Celtic, they were friends. Liam found himself laughing and cheering along with them.

When training was over, Liam helped the rest of the lads gather the cones and footballs and carry them to the clubhouse for Coach Billy. The team fist-bumped each other, and Liam thanked every player on the squad.

"We've our last pre-season friendly on Saturday," said Coach Billy just as Liam was about to leave. "Come down if you want to play. 11am kick-off, here at the Hawk's Nest."

"The Hawk's Nest?" asked Liam.

Billy shrugged. "Yeah, that's what we call the pitches here. Our home ground."

"OK, great. Thanks, Billy."

Liam strode to Mum's car as though he walked on a cushion of air. He opened the door and sat inside.

"Well?" asked Mum. "How was it?"

"So much fun, Mum," said Liam. "I think I'm going to like this team." For the first time since setting foot in England, Liam felt like he had something to be genuinely happy about.

CHAPTER NINE

TOM

The day after training, Tom walked to school with Jake and endured English, science, and religious studies classes. They played football at lunchtime, and the new lad Liam joined in and scored a hat-trick of impressive goals. The rest of Tom's first week at school passed by in much the same way. Lessons, football at lunchtime, and then playing with his friends in the area where they lived. Tom lived in a housing estate a five-minute cycle away from the Hawk's Nest. His estate was a tangle of winding streets, where most of his teammates lived in a mix of different-sized houses and flats. Tom lived in a semi-detached house with his mum and older brother, Ian.

On Wednesday evening, Tom walked home as usual and used his key to open his front door. The front garden was little more than a scrap of grass in desperate need of cutting, and a conifer tree shaped like a giant green triangle. Tom entered the house and closed the door behind him. His mum worked as a hairdresser five days per week, but she always left some food for Tom and his brother to eat after school. He left his bag in the hall, poked his head into the fridge, found nothing, and then went to the hob cooker, where he found a pot of tomato and basil pasta. Tom grabbed a spoon, scooped half of the pasta into a bowl, and popped it into the microwave for a minute.

The microwave turned with its familiar mechanical sound, and Tom poured himself a glass of blackcurrant. A loud ping let him know the food was ready, and he took it out of the microwave, using a towel to protect his hands from the hot bowl. He placed it on the kitchen table and grabbed his homework folder from his schoolbag. Tom spooned a forkful of pasta into his mouth and took out his maths homework. The pasta was red hot and a piece of it slipped out of his mouth like a snake and plopped right into the middle of his homework book. He grabbed it, but not quickly enough to avoid a nasty red smear on the page where he had to answer a dozen long division questions.

Tom ate his pasta and tried to do his homework around the pasta smear. He was almost finished when the front door opened and slammed shut.

"Hiya, worm," said Ian as he bundled into the

kitchen, floppy hair hanging over his eyes and white earpods stuffed into each ear. "What's cooking?"

"Pasta," replied Tom. Ian was four years older than Tom. He was lanky and about a million times cooler than Tom thought he could ever be.

"Again?" Ian opened every cupboard in the house in search of something different. He found a can of soup, checked the best-before date, sighed and tossed it into the bin. "Pasta it is, then."

"Mum does her best."

"I know she does." Ian heated his own bowl of pasta and sat on the table in the seat opposite Tom. "It ain't easy bringing up a worm like you on her own."

"At least I make my own bed."

"What happened to your homework? Shall I get you a bib?"

"Shut up, lanky. Have you got a match this weekend?"

"Yeah. Friendly on Sunday, then the league starts next week. Have you?" Ian played for Hawk FC, four years ahead of Tom.

"Friendly on Saturday."

"I'll come down and cheer you on, worm."

Tom smiled. Even though his brother teased him mercilessly, he always looked out for him. They both finished their pasta and washed up their bowls. They had chores to do before their mum came home, so Tom hoovered downstairs whilst Ian took some washing out of the machine and hung the clothes out to dry. Tom hated doing chores, but he and Ian had to help their mum run the house. As he pushed the hoover around the sitting-room carpet, Tom thought about the new season and hoped that Hawk could at least win a few matches. Relegation would be humiliating, and it would be a long season if they were going to get hammered every week.

CHAPTER TEN

LIAM

On the morning after training with Hawk FC, Liam walked to school as normal. The blazer which had caused so much embarrassment on his first day was firmly banished to the wardrobe at home, and Liam now wore a jumper over his school shirt and tie, along with the too-large trousers. He left his estate and followed the same route as he had all week. As he crossed the road and entered the long road leading to school, his eyes darted to every corner, beneath every tree and searched both in front and behind him for any sign of Jax and the Darkstone bullies. The way ahead seemed clear, so Liam quickened his pace towards the school gates.

Liam weaved in and out of the crowd of kids, all making their way down the road towards school like him. Some walked on the pavements, and others along the road itself. A row of big, detached houses with curving pathways and pretty gardens lined one side of the road, and on the other stretched the rear of a factory with old wooden pallets and empty crates packed haphazardly outside. Liam ducked beneath the arms of an older boy busy waving them around as he talked to his friends. He darted around a group of girls listening to blaring music from an iPhone. Liam saw a gap and ran into it, trying to get into school and to his first class without bumping into the Darkstone Rangers boys.

A boy crashed into him from the side, almost knocking Liam off his feet. The boy apologised and held up a small American football that he and his friends were throwing to each other. Liam smiled to say it was OK and turned back towards the school to find himself face-to-face with Jax.

"Well, well," Jax smirked, a nasty smile splitting his face. "Look what I've found, boys."

"A muppet!" crowed another spiteful voice, and six of the Darkstone boys appeared behind Jax, all glowering at Liam.

Liam took a step back, but it was too late to run.

"Where are you going?" Jax shot out a hand, grabbed a fistful of Liam's jumper and dragged him close. "I haven't got you back yet for poking me in the eye. What shall we do to him, lads? I need payback."

"Take his shoes and throw them in the bin," suggested one Ranger.

"Empty his bag again," another chimed in.

"Take off his trousers and leave him in just his undies for the day," sniggered a third, and Liam's stomach churned with fear.

"Liam!" called a voice, and Liam turned to see Tom and a few of the Hawk FC boys coming down the road. "Everything OK?" It was Jake, the team's centre-back.

"Get lost, Chicken FC," said Jax, and his friends laughed at his joke, high-fiving each other and pointing at the Hawk FC boys.

"Leave him alone, Jax," said Tom. More of the Hawk FC boys emerged from the crowd until there were nine boys Liam recognised from the team.

Jax pushed Liam away and curled his lip. "Your time will come, muppet," he threatened. The Darkstone players turned and carried on towards school, making chicken noises and hooting with laughter.

"They've got it in for you big time," said Tom. "Try to keep away from them. They have a bad reputation. The teacher threw Jax out of English class yesterday for being cheeky. But if the Darkstone lot gives you any more trouble, remember that we're your teammates now. That doesn't just mean we play for the same team. It means we are mates on and off the pitch. If someone does something mean to one of us, they do it to all of us."

"Us Hawks stick together," said John, draping his arm around Liam's shoulder.

"Thanks, lads." Liam's voice trembled as he spoke. "I am trying to keep away from them. But they just keep turning up like that one sock without its pair at the bottom of your sock drawer."

"You're going to have to stand up to them eventually," said Jake. "We've got them the first game of the season."

"Hawk FC are playing Darkstone Rangers?" Liam couldn't believe it. He hadn't even signed for Hawk yet, and already they had a nightmare game coming up.

"Yep," nodded Tom. "We've a friendly this weekend, and then Darkstone next Saturday."

They set off towards school with Liam in their midst. Even though Liam was afraid of Jax and his friends, he knew he couldn't run away from them forever. Jake was right. Eventually, he would have to stand up to them, or they would just keep on bullying him forever. Being brave like that was easier said than done, however, and Liam hoped he could find enough courage to play his best game against them. But first, he had to play on Saturday and play well. Then he could sign for Hawk. Even if that meant playing a match against his worst enemies in his first game of the season.

CHAPTER ELEVEN

TOM

Saturday morning came around quickly and Tom awoke excited to play the friendly Coach Billy had arranged against Beavis Sports, a team in the league below Hawk FC.

"What would you like for breakfast, love?" asked Tom's mum when he came downstairs. Saturday was her day off, and Tom gave her a big hug.

"Have we got any eggs?" he said, scratching at his hair, which stuck up in wild clumps from a night in bed.

"Ah. Of course, you've got a match today. Scrambled eggs, is it?"

"Yes, please, Mum." Tom always ate scrambled eggs and toast the morning of a game. It gave him energy.

Mum made the eggs and brought them to Tom, who was waiting at the kitchen table. She kissed him on the head as she carefully laid the plate down before him.

"I'm going to come and watch you today. I can't wait."

"Thanks, Mum." Tom finished his breakfast and went upstairs to get ready for the match.

Tom arrived at the Hawk's Nest at 10.30am for the warm-up. The sun shone bright in a cloudless sky the colour of Manchester City's home kit. A light late summer's breeze drifted across the Hawk's Nest to flutter the four corner flags. All the lads were there, including the new boy, Liam. After the stretching, Billy told the boys to practise shooting against Mark, the goalkeeper. Billy trudged off the sideline and the lads all took turns taking shots. The other team arrived wearing a blue kit. As kick-off drew near, Billy waved the team over and handed out the jerseys. Hawk FC played in yellow jerseys, which seemed almost golden on sunny days, green shorts, and green and gold striped socks. The kit was a hand-me-down from previous Hawk FC teams. It was faded and worn, and some jerseys were even ripped in places. The kit was old and tattered, but it was Hawk FC and every time Tom pulled it on, he felt like a knight putting on a suit of armour.

"Usual set-up today," announced Billy, his voice flat and distant. "Sergio is still injured, so Liam is going to come in and play striker."

"Don't you play in midfield?" asked Tom, turning to Liam.

"I'll play anywhere," Liam said and shrugged his shoulders.

The referee blew the whistle, and the team lined up. Jake and Big Dave at the back, with Tom at right-back and Leo in front of him at right-wing.

"Are you ready for this, Leo?" Tom shouted up the wing to where Leo was playing with the string from his shorts.

"What? Me?" Leo called back. "Ready for what?"

"For the match, Leo! Switch on, mate!"

The whistle blew for kick-off and Beavis Sports kicked the ball around their midfielders. Liam set off like a cheetah, chasing them down and winning the ball with his first tackle. It took the Hawk FC players by surprise, and they suddenly sprang to life. Adam charged from centre midfield, received a pass from Liam, and gave it back to him in a quick one-two. Liam did a step-over, and completely sent the Beavis centre-back to the shops. He went one way and Liam went the other. He was one-on-one with the goalkeeper and squared the ball to Adam, who went to shoot, missed the ball completely and fell over. Tom knew it was too good to be true.

"Well done, boys," shouted Big Dave, clapping his

hands. "Let's go again!"

The ball came long from a goal kick, heading straight towards Tom. He braced himself and headed the ball away. He caught it clean with his forehead and the ball bounced in front of Leo. Leo swung a leg at it, but the Beavis winger nipped in front of him and crossed the ball first time into their striker. He was a tall boy with long hair tied back in a ponytail. The striker took the ball on his chest and volleyed it into the top corner of the goal before Big Dave or Jake could do anything about it. One–nil.

CHAPTER TWELVE

LIAM

Hawk FC was three-nil down at half-time. It was a warm September morning, and dew clung to the newly mown grass, leaving the playing surface slick and quick. Beavis Sports moved the ball around well, but Liam had played much better teams back home in Ireland. The lads used the half-time break to grab a drink of water and catch their breath. The Hawk FC jersey had long sleeves, and Liam rolled his up to the elbows to cool himself down. He liked the yellow-gold colour. It was bright, but it looked superb with the green shorts and striped socks. The kit was old and faded, like someone had bought it from a second-hand shop. It was a bit like Hawk FC itself, rough around the edges, in need of something new, but it was honest and stood for something Liam could really believe in. Some lads had half-zip training tops with the same colours and the club badge, and Liam thought he would ask Mum to get him one.

The smell of the freshly cut grass filled his nose, and even though his team was losing, Liam felt brilliant. His heart beat fast in his chest from the exertion of running around the pitch. Mud streaked his knees from a slide tackle in the first half, and sweat plastered his hair on his forehead. He loved football and playing again made him feel alive, like he was his old self again.

"Unlucky, lads," said Coach Billy. "We've had a few quality chances. Liam, well done, lad."

"We need to keep it tight," said Tom.

"Start passing the ball around," added Jake.

"Try to get the ball over the top to me," Liam said after he had taken a long drink. "I think I'm faster than both of their centre-backs."

"Get it to Liam, lads," ordered Big Dave, wiping sweat from his face onto the sleeve of his jersey. "We have to win. This lot are in the league below us. If we can't beat them, what chance do we have of beating anybody in our own league?"

Liam took another drink and pulled up his socks. Hawk FC had a few talented players. Tom could play, and so could Jake. Big Dave wasn't the best with the ball, but he was useful in the air and was as strong as a bull. Between them, they would have to find a way to win. The referee blew his whistle. It was time for the second half, and it was Hawk FC's kick-off. Liam took the ball and placed it on the white-washed centre circle. He passed the ball back to Tom at right-back, turned, and set off running towards the goal.

Liam scanned his opposition to check their positions, turned over his shoulder and saw Tom clip the ball high over the midfield. It came towards him, and Liam sensed the Beavis centre-back coming to head the ball. Liam jumped and flicked the ball on with his head. He landed, crashed into the charging defender, and almost lost his balance. Liam staggered, fell to one knee, and forced himself to stay standing up. He bunched his leg muscles and sprang into an all-out sprint. The Beavis keeper ran from his box, trying to intercept the bouncing ball, and the last defender charged towards it from the left.

Liam sprinted, pumping his arms, gritting his teeth, determined to get there first. All the other sounds around him fell silent. The shouts of support from the sidelines, the thud of football boots on the grass, the calls of his teammates and of the opposition. All Liam could hear was the bounce of the ball and his own breath. He ran as fast as he possibly could. The goalkeeper dived at the ball feet first, and for a terrible moment, Liam thought the goalie would get there first and completely take him out. But Liam's legs drove him forward, and he made it to the ball just before the goalie. Liam poked his left foot at the ball, pushing it wide of the goalkeeper, whose facial expression turned from determined focus to surprised regret. The goalie's mouth fell open and his eyes clamped shut as the goalie crashed into his own centre-back. Liam left them in a tangled heap of legs, arms, and football boots and passed the ball into the goal. Three-one!

Sound rushed back into Liam's ears, and he jumped for joy. As the sideline clapped, he turned to see his teammates hurtling towards him with smiles splitting their faces. He opened his arms and welcomed them in.

"What a goal!" whooped Paulie, the centre-midfielder.

"Let's go, Liam!" cheered Jake, and he ruffled Liam's hair.

They set up again for kick-off, and Beavis came at them, putting together a string of deft passes which took them through the midfield until Big Dave came crashing in and won the ball with a fair shoulder into the Beavis striker.

The game swung one way and then the other, but the Hawks found it difficult to get the ball through to Liam. Passes came his way, but they were either too short and the defenders kicked them away, or too long and bounced out of touch. Liam got one more shot away. He tackled the Beavis left-back and curled a shot, which the Beavis keeper tipped over his own bar.

The game ended and the Hawk FC lads dropped to their knees with exhaustion. Beavis Sports leapt with joy and ran about the pitch in celebration. It was only a friendly, but Beavis had beaten a team from the league above them, so it was an enormous victory.

"I can't believe we lost that," panted Adam, coming to stand next to Liam.

"We can't pass the ball," groaned Jake, shaking his head. "We can't tackle. What chance have we got when we play Darkstone next week?"

"We've got Liam now," said Tom. "He's a talented player. We can improve."

"Not by doing the same drills over and again every week, we can't," sighed Leo, and everybody turned to look at the right-winger who normally had his head firmly set in the clouds but, for once, had spoken the truth.

CHAPTER THIRTEEN

TOM

Tom rode his bike to training on Tuesday night, thinking over the defeat against Beavis Sports and how the team could improve. It was all he and Jake had spoken about since the match. At school lunchtime on both Monday and Tuesday, the team met and discussed tactics, trying to find a way not to get absolutely hammered by Darkstone Rangers. The houses and streets whipped by as Tom turned the pedals and steered his bike around the lanes and streets.

He reached the Hawk's Nest just as a light rain whipped about the fields. Tom climbed off his bike, took his backpack off, and fished out his training rain-jacket. He pulled it on and joined the lads who huddled beside the clubhouse.

"If we do the same old thing, we'll get battered on

he loved it. He might not know the latest tactics or fancy training drills, but he loved the lads and the club, and there was something important about that.

"Come on," Tom said to the rest of the boys. "Stretches and laps."

The team followed Tom onto the pitch and stretched out their hamstrings. Billy set down the bag of balls and began to lay the cones out for the usual passing drill. He glanced at Tom and smiled, saying thanks without speaking. Tom returned the smile.

Some things are more important than winning, he thought. He moved through the stretches and wondered if he would feel the same way on Saturday when they had to play Darkstone Rangers.

CHAPTER FOURTEEN

LIAM

The week went by in a blur, and Saturday came around quickly. Liam avoided Jax and his Darkstone Rangers friends and spent his days hanging around with his new teammates. He found he was actually starting to enjoy school. Liam played football at lunchtime and had at least one Hawk FC player in every class. He and Ronan talked on a video call on Friday night, and Liam told him all about Hawk FC and Ronan let Liam know everything going on back in Ireland.

For the first time since Liam had arrived in England, he'd had an enjoyable week. He woke happy on Saturday until he remembered today he would play his first league game for Hawk FC, and that game was against Darkstone Rangers. His stomach felt hollow and all he wanted to do was pull the duvet over his head and stay in bed. But it was game day, and his teammates needed him, so Liam got out of bed, went downstairs, and ate his breakfast. He checked his boots, shin pads, shorts and socks and got himself ready for the game.

"Can't wait to see you play today, son," said Dad as they got into the car to leave for the game.

"It's going to be a tough one," said Liam as he fastened his seatbelt.

"I'm sorry I've been so busy with work. We haven't got to spend much time together since we moved."

"It's all right, Dad."

"Mum is taking Penny to gymnastics today, so we can grab some lunch after the match if you like. Just me and you."

"Thanks, Dad, that sounds great." Liam stared out of the window as Dad started the car. He wondered if he should tell him about Jax and the problems at school, but Dad seemed so happy about the game and Liam didn't want to spoil it. So, he watched the houses and shops zip by as the car twisted and turned until they reached the Hawk's Nest.

"Good luck," said Dad as Liam got out of the car. They bumped fists and Liam walked to join the lads inside the clubhouse changing room.

Liam pulled open the door and immediately the aroma of old sweat, stinky football boots, damp walls and mud assaulted his senses. The smell of football. He walked into the changing room to find most of the team already there. They greeted him with high-fives and fist-bumps and Liam sat down next to Tom.

"Are you ready for today?" asked Tom.

Liam shrugged. "Ready as I'll ever be."

Coach Billy came bustling into the changing room and dropped the kit bag onto the floor with a thud. He pulled a crumpled piece of paper out of his pocket, squinted, brought the paper close to his face, and read out the team.

"Mark in goal," Billy announced. "Jake and Big Dave centre-backs. Tom right-back and Pardeep at left-back. Adam and Paulie centre-midfield. Leo right-wing, Carl left-wing. John defensive midfield and Liam up top."

Billy handed out the jerseys and tossed the number ten to Liam. He pulled it on, and even with the hole beneath the left armpit and the bottom part of the number one missing, it felt great to put on the Hawk FC kit. It made Liam feel part of something, like he was in an army getting ready to fight a battle. Butterflies fluttered in his stomach, nervous at the thought of facing his bullies on the football pitch.

"Everybody in," gestured Tom. The team gathered about him in a huddle. Liam put his arm around Tom's shoulders, and Big Dave wrapped his heavy arm around Liam's shoulders as they all came together as one. "Play for each other today. Play for Hawk FC. No matter what the score is, try to enjoy it. Let's do our best. Who are we?"

"Hawk FC!" roared the rest of the team at the same time. They stomped their boots on the cracked wooden floor, and the noise sounded like thunder in the small changing room. Tom led them out, and they ran out of the clubhouse onto the grass where the Darkstone Rangers waited for them wearing their all-black kit. Every one of them was tall and broad-shouldered, their faces hard like stone. Liam gulped and his heart skipped a beat as Jax glared at him and shook his head. He looked Liam up and down, whispered something to the rest of the Darkstone team, and they sniggered. It was time for Liam to face his enemies, and he hoped they wouldn't smash him to pieces.

CHAPTER FIFTEEN

LIAM

Liam took his place on the edge of the centre circle for kick-off.

"Crush them! Hurt them! Beat them! Own them!" the Darkstone Rangers team shouted as one.

The sound of that chilling mantra shook Liam like a punch to his gut. The Darkstone Rangers broke from their huddle and took up their formation on the pitch. Jax strolled towards Liam and ran a hand through his red hair.

"Nice kit, loser," Jax sneered. He glanced down at the faded Hawk FC jersey and shook his head. "I'm going to two-foot you today."

Liam just stared back at him, unable to find anything clever to say, petrified that the entire Darkstone team was out to get him. The whistle blew, and the match was underway. The Darkstone striker passed the ball back to Buzz Cut, who passed it to Jax. Liam tried to get in front of him and steal the ball, but Jax thundered a shoulder into him. It was like being kicked by a horse and Liam fell to the ground as Jax turned away, sprinting towards the goal. He dribbled past Adam and was almost through on goal until Big Dave tackled him and kicked the ball out of play.

The first half passed Liam by in a blur of black shirts. He found himself running around in the opposition's half but unable to get a touch of the ball. The Hawk FC players tried to hit it long, but it was as though Liam was smaller, slower, and not as good as the Darkstone players. He was second to every pass, every header and every tackle. Tom, Jake, Pardeep and Dave played well at the back and kept Darkstone out until the tenth minute, when Jax hit a shot from outside of the box and it flew into the top corner like a bullet. He celebrated like Jude Bellingham with his arms outstretched, staring straight into Liam's eyes.

Three more goals went in before the referee blew for half-time. Sergio stood beside Coach Billy on the sideline, hopping about on his crutches and shouting support to the team. It was a relief when the first half ended. Liam had got through it without getting hurt, and as he turned to leave the pitch, Jax ran over to him.

"Hawk FC is a joke," Jax jeered, and poked a thick

finger into Liam's chest. "The clubhouse is a wreck, the team is weak, and you are their worst player. I can't wait to see you get relegated."

Without saying a word, Liam ran away from him and joined his teammates on the sideline.

"Keep it tight, lads," Coach Billy encouraged. "We can get back into this game. Keep doing your best."

"We're getting hammered, Billy," said John. "All you ever say is keep it tight. Give us some ideas about how we can score a goal."

"That's enough of that talk," Tom said. "We need to be brave. Get our feet on the ball and start passing it. Liam, I know Jax is giving you a tough time, but you need to get your head in the game. You're a great player, and we need you."

Liam took a drink from his water bottle and thought about that. Jax and his friends had done their best to make his life a misery. Liam knew that everything Tom said was right, but the thought of playing against Darkstone filled him with fear.

Liam took the second half kick-off and passed the ball back to Paulie in midfield. Liam turned and made a run, and Paulie kicked a through ball which was too short and not powerful enough for him to run on to. He chased after it and just before he got his foot on the ball, Jax came sliding in. It was an awful tackle. Two feet outstretched, legs in the air, nowhere near the ball. Jax's boots clattered through

Liam's shins like a hammer. He cried out and fell, rolling onto the wet grass.

"Told you I would get you," panted Jax as he got back to his feet. The referee blew for a free kick and showed Jax a yellow card.

Liam's shins burned like fire. He lay on the ground, holding back tears, not wanting to give Jax the satisfaction of seeing him cry. Tom and John helped him to his feet, and Liam limped into the box as Tom took the free kick. He hit a good cross into the box, but it sailed over Liam's head because he couldn't jump for the header. The Darkstone boys jostled him in the box, pushing and laughing at him. It was like Liam's first day of school all over again.

The second half continued in the same way as the first. The Hawk FC players struggled to control the ball. They misplaced passes and Darkstone took advantage of every mistake. Jax scored another goal, followed by two more in quick succession. Jake put a crunching tackle in on a Darkstone player and they gathered around him, pushing and shouting at him until the referee waved them all away.

"You lot are an embarrassment," taunted Jax as the Hawk FC players came to help Jake, pulling him away from the Darkstone team. "You should be ashamed to play for this joke of a team!"

"I bet we beat you in the next game," yelled Tom, his face red with anger.

"Oh yeah? Bet what?"

Tom realised what he had said, and the colour drained from his face. "I bet we beat you at your ground. If we win, you wash our kit and clean our boots."

"All right then." Jax rubbed his hands together. "But if we beat you at home, you guys agree not to play again for the rest of the season until you are relegated. Also, every one of you has to kiss the Darkstone badge before you leave the field."

"You've got a deal," said Big Dave, and he shook Jax's hand so hard that he almost pulled the Darkstone player to the floor.

Jax laughed and ran to his teammates.

"Oh no," Tom whispered. "What have I done?"

"No time to worry about it now," said Liam. "We have to finish this game first."

"We're in it together," said Big Dave. "Always."

The second half was a complete disaster and Darkstone won seven-nil. Liam trudged from the pitch with his head held low. It was the worst game he had ever played, and his enemies had got the better of him again. The Hawk FC players collected their bags from the changing rooms in silence, shocked by the terrible defeat, but also at the bet they were all now committed to. As he walked to Dad's car, all Liam could think about was how humiliating it would be if they had to forfeit the season and be relegated, and then kiss the Darkstone badge. The thought of it filled Liam with sickening fear and he wondered if football would ever be fun again.

CHAPTER SIXTEEN

TOM

"What were you thinking?" exclaimed Adam at training three days after the defeat by Darkstone Rangers. "It was a crazy bet to make!"

"I wasn't thinking at all!" Tom hung his head in despair. "The looks on their smug faces just annoyed me. It just came out of my mouth before I knew what I was saying." Which was true. Tom had spent every moment since the match regretting the bet with Jax.

"Do we really have to kiss their badge if we lose?" asked Liam.

"Yep," Jake replied. "That's bad enough, but we'll also forfeit every game after that until we're relegated to the second division."

"There's no point moaning about it now," said Big Dave. "We are Hawk FC. What we need to do is get better and beat them."

"Easier said than done," said Paulie. He was a tall boy with long hair hanging loose about his shoulders.

"Here's Coach Billy," said Liam. "Let's see what he has to say about it."

"Probably not much," muttered Mark, and he was rewarded with a scowl from Tom.

"OK, boys," said Coach Billy. "Stretches and laps. Are we ready?"

Tom hated to put Billy on the spot, but he had no choice. This was serious now. It was about the team, his friends, and not being humiliated by Darkstone Rangers.

"Coach Billy?" Tom said, and every player on the team turned and looked at him. "We have to get better. We have to find a way to beat Darkstone Rangers."

"Hard work and teamwork," said Billy brightly and walked towards the pitch.

"No, Coach. We want to do something else. Work on tactics. Improve." Tom winced as the words left his mouth. Billy turned and his expression changed from his usual excitement about training and having fun with the team to a saggy-faced stare.

"I've already taught you boys everything I know." Billy set down the balls and cones. "It isn't always about winning, Tom."

"I know, Billy. But this time it is. We must win that game."

Billy itched his white chin stubble and nodded. His face changed from sadness to a clever grin. He wagged his finger at Tom. "I knew this day would come. When you boys would outgrow old Billy. Leave it with me, boys. I have a plan. We'll do the usual session tonight, but be ready to crank things up a notch next time."

Tom was surprised and excited to hear Billy talk about a fresh approach. But he couldn't help feeling like he had hurt Billy's feelings. After training was over, Tom waited on his bike outside the clubhouse until he heard Billy come whistling to the door to turn the lights off.

"Oh, hello, Tom," said Coach Billy as he stepped outside and put his keys in the clubhouse door. "Why are you still here? You should be at home having your dinner by now."

"I know, Coach Billy, I just wanted to say that I'm sorry," said Tom. He stared at the grass, unable to meet Billy's eyes.

"You're a great lad, Tom. You've got nothing to be sorry for."

"For speaking up earlier. I didn't mean to make you feel bad."

Billy laughed. He locked the door and walked slowly over to Tom. He smiled and wagged a crooked finger. "I want you boys to be able to speak your minds. That is what this club is all about: friendship and respect. Our results weren't so good last season, and we are struggling this season. You are right. We need something fresh. I've just the thing. Leave it to old Billy."

"Don't leave us though, Coach. It wouldn't be the same without you."

"I won't be going anywhere, laddie. You might not know this, but I live on my own. This club is all I've got. Training you boys is the best part of my week. But I owe it to you to improve the team. What you also might not know is that I used to be in the army."

"Really?" Tom had only ever thought of Billy as he was now, grey-haired and happy-faced. He had given no thought to what Billy might have been like as a younger man.

"Yes, I was a soldier for fifteen years. I saw the world. So, believe me when I say I know what it means to want to win and want to be the best. I won't let you down, Tom. Sometimes in life, we let things get easy. We don't try our hardest and think that doing the minimum is enough. But it isn't. If you want to do well in your exams and have a decent job when you leave school, you need to focus to make sure you do your homework and concentrate in class and study hard. Or if you want to improve at football, you need to use the time at training to put maximum effort in. Jogging around and joking with your mates isn't enough. So, from now on, we'll train harder. Much harder.

"But you've also got to think about what you can do personally to improve your game. It can't always be down to someone else to do things for you. You must take responsibility for your own performance. Do you do extra ball work at home? Practice keep-ups and do left and right foot passing against a wall every day? Do you do sit-ups and press-ups to strengthen yourself? I don't want you to answer those questions, Tom, but think about them on your way home. I'll see you on Thursday for training."

CHAPTER SEVENTEEN

LIAM

The day after training, Liam sat in English class listening to his teacher talk about Private Peaceful, a book Liam and the rest of the class had to read before the end of term. He sat next to Leo, the Hawk FC right-winger, but Leo barely spoke during the lesson. In fact, Leo barely spoke at all. He just stared out of the window and was, without a doubt, the most relaxed person Liam had met in his entire life.

The bell rang, and it was time to go to his next lesson. Liam packed up his things, said goodbye to Leo, and headed out into the corridor. He left the classroom and went out into the mass of students packed into the corridor, each one making their way to the second lesson of the day. He was about to make a right turn towards the maths rooms when a hand grabbed him from behind and bundled him into an empty classroom.

"Hey!" exclaimed Liam, at first thinking it was one of the Hawk FC lads playing a joke on him.

"Hello, muppet," came a familiar voice. One that made Liam's shoulders shiver. It was Jax.

Liam turned to run for the door, but Buzz Cut slammed it closed and blocked it with his body. Six more Darkstone players stood around Liam, closing in to make a tight circle. Liam's stomach clenched, and he was suddenly extremely thirsty.

"Leave me alone," Liam said, staring at each boy. "I have done nothing to you. Let me go."

"You poked me in the eye," said Jax.

"And you clattered me in the match on Saturday. So, we're even."

"I say when we are even. And we are not. Hold him."

Strong hands grabbed Liam around the arms and chest. He bucked and kicked like a wild horse trying to get away from them, but the Darkstone players were too many and too strong. Jax pulled a large pair of scissors from his bag and snipped them in front of Liam's face. Liam cried out and turned away, but his enemies gripped him in place.

"You don't have your useless teammates to help you now, do you? No sign of Big Dave to get you out of trouble?"

"Stop it! Let me go!"

Jax pulled out Liam's tie and cut it with the scissors. He dangled the cut piece in front of Liam's face and the other Darkstone boys laughed, eyes wide with glee as Liam suffered. Next, Jax cut the laces out of Liam's shoes and was about to take the scissors to Liam's trousers before Buzz Cut stopped him.

"All right Jax," he said. "You've got your own back. That's enough now."

"I say when it's enough," Jax snarled.

Buzz Cut pulled Liam out of the circle and opened the door.

"Go," he urged.

Liam made a run for it and left the classroom as though he were running through on goal. Tears streamed down his face and Liam didn't know what to do. He ran until he found the PE changing room and ducked inside. Thankfully, the changing room was empty, and he slumped onto a chair with his head in his hands. Liam couldn't let things go on like this. He wiped his tears away and stood, staring at himself in the changing room mirror.

I won't let them do this to me anymore, he thought. *I am a good footballer. I can stand up for myself.*

Things had to change. Liam knew at that moment he wouldn't run from his bullies ever again.

CHAPTER EIGHTEEN

TOM

"You're lucky you had a spare tie at home," said Tom as they waited for Thursday training to start.

"I know," agreed Liam. "My mum would have gone crazy. She would have gone into school and complained about Jax to the teachers."

"Maybe that would have been for the best?"

"It wouldn't have stopped it. I have to put a stop to Jax and the Darkstone boys myself."

"Fair play to you, Liam," said Big Dave, and he gave Liam a fist-bump. "We could stand up for you. I could get Jax on his own and make him understand the error of his ways. But if you don't stop them, there will always be more bullies. Sometimes you just have to stand up for yourself."

The rest of the team nodded their agreement, and Tom was surprised because people rarely turned to Big Dave for words of wisdom. Big and brutally strong, yes. Calm and full of useful advice, not so much. Tom had arrived at the clubhouse for Thursday training early, eager to see what Coach Billy had come up with to help the team improve before their showdown with Darkstone Rangers later in the season.

Every player on the team arrived at the Hawk's Nest ten minutes early, even Leo, who came with his boots on, laces tied, actually looking excited to train. The clubhouse door opened, and Coach Billy walked out, carrying the bag of balls and stack of cones the same as he did at every training session. Tom's heart sank, and he crossed his fingers behind his back, hoping that Billy would not send them off to stretch, run laps, and then start a passing drill.

"Good evening, lads," Coach Billy greeted them. Tom could almost feel the sighs of disappointment from every boy on the team as their shoulders slumped. They all just wanted to get better. To win. To play decent football.

The clubhouse door creaked open again, and a man strode out wearing a coach's tracksuit bottoms and a skin-tight Under Armour top. A whistle rested against his chest and muscles rippled across his arms as he stood next to Coach Billy.

He's young, perhaps thirty, Tom thought. He had a

square jaw, short spiky hair, and bright blue piercing eyes the colour of a frozen lake.

"This is my nephew, Jimmy," grinned Coach Billy. "Until recently, he coached Liverpool's reserves. He's looking for a new coaching job, but in the meantime, he's going to coach Hawk FC. He knows what he's doing. If you want to get better, do what he says."

Tom's mouth gaped open, as wide as a cave, and he stared at Jimmy.

"Liverpool's reserve coach!" Jake whispered in Tom's ear. "I can't believe it!"

Tom tried to speak, but his mouth just flapped open and closed like a fish. His heart beat faster because it might finally happen. They might actually start to play good football!

"OK, boys!" Jimmy's voice was clear and crisp. "We'll start with a warm-up."

Jimmy laid out lines of cones and let the lads run between them in distinct patterns. They ran, jumped to head an imaginary ball, ran backwards, and even jumped into each other with their shoulders as they zigzagged through the cones.

"Remember to call your name," Jimmy instructed as the boys jumped in the air and made a heading motion. "Call your name every time you jump to head the ball."

It was Tom's turn and as he leapt into the air, he

shouted, "Tom's ball!"

"Good, well done," praised Jimmy, and Tom's chest burned with pride.

Jimmy got them together in a huddle after the warm-up. "As the weeks go on, I'll work with you on ball control, passing and shooting. But first, we need to get the basics right. This week, it's defending."

The team spent the next hour learning how to pass the ball out from the back. Mark, the goalie, would give Tom a short pass, and he would try to find a midfielder or a winger with his second touch. Then Jimmy added in attackers, and they had to go over, and over the practice, until Jimmy was happy, they could get it right. Coach Billy watched from the sidelines with a proud smile on his face. He encouraged the lads, clapped every goal, and admired every tackle.

"If we can pass the ball through their lines and get it into our attackers, we can create chances to score," Jimmy said. "Next, let's learn how to defend."

Jimmy taught the team how to delay an attacker, jockey a runner, and then put a foot in at the right time. He taught them how to stay goal-side of an attacker, use their shoulders, and slide tackle. Every boy on the Hawk FC team was dripping with sweat at the end of the session. Tom rode his bike home with his head swimming with all he had learned. Maybe, just maybe, if they played using the skills

Jimmy had taught them, Hawk FC might win a match.

CHAPTER NINETEEN

LIAM

Liam waited at the school gates wearing his spare tie, with laces from an old pair of trainers in his school shoes. He had hardly slept last night, playing over and over in his head what he had to do today and how it might go. He had woken sweating from a terrible nightmare in which Jax had flushed his head down the toilet. That was the worst-case scenario. But Liam had to confront his problems, and it had to be today.

He noticed a shock of red hair bobbing amongst the crowd of children making their way up the street to school. It was Jax, surrounded as usual by half of the Darkstone Rangers' team. Liam's stomach tightened, and he stuffed sweaty hands into his pockets. His brain told him to turn and run, forget his plan, and get away from his bullies, but his heart forced him to stay.

The Darkstone Rangers came closer, and Liam saw Big Dave, Tom, Jake and Mark waiting across the road from the corner of his eye. He glanced at them, and Big Dave nodded and winked at him. Liam hadn't known they would be there. Perhaps they had seen him waiting and knew what was about to happen. He was glad they were there, but Liam had to do this alone.

"Snip, snip," Jax mocked with a sly grin as he approached the gates. He stared at Liam with a look of triumph in his eyes. "Good of you to wait here for your daily punishment, muppet. Nice tie. It would be a shame if I had to cut it again."

Liam stood up straight as the Darkstone Rangers gathered about him. "You started this thing, Jax, not me," Liam said. "What you did to me yesterday was out of order. It's gone too far. Instead of standing behind your friends and bullying me, why don't we just settle this on the pitch? We have our bet and when we play at your ground, one team will win, and one will lose."

"I can't wait to see you lot go down. Chicken FC." Jax turned to his mates, who all laughed just as he expected them to. "I want a picture when you have to kiss the Darkstone badge. We can put it up in our clubhouse. Perhaps they'll print it in the local paper?"

"If you lose, you must wash our kit and clean our boots. That's the deal. So, leave me alone until then. Let us prepare properly for the match. No more attacking me in the corridors."

"I already told you, muppet." Jax poked his finger sharply into Liam's chest. "I decide when it's over. I wonder what it will be today? Maybe I'll take your lunch. Or your shoes."

"Do you take pleasure in being cruel? We're both footballers. Settle this on the pitch, unless you're scared?"

"Me? Scared?" Jax pushed Liam in the chest, and he stumbled backwards.

Liam feared the worst. He panicked, fearing that Jax was about to beat him up. To Tom's surprise, Buzz Cut stepped in front of Jax.

"That's enough," he said, staring up into Jax's angry eyes. "He's right. Leave it now. We'll settle it on the pitch." He glanced at Liam, and there was a sad look in his eyes, as though he knew that Jax's bullying was out of line.

Jax spluttered, looked around at his teammates, and they all looked away. They agreed with Buzz Cut. "All right then, muppet," Jax snarled, pointing at Liam. "We'll leave you be until the match."

Liam wanted to thank Buzz Cut, but he thought better of it and just stood his ground. He was about to turn and leave, relieved that it was over, but then Jax spoke and stopped him in his tracks.

"On one condition. Let's make the bet a bit more personal. If Darkstone beat Hawk FC, you have to quit football. Just you. Toss your boots in the bin and never play again."

Liam swallowed hard. "But if Hawk wins, you never come near me again. Ever."

"Deal." A snake-like grin spread across Jax's face, and he strode away with his teammates surrounding him.

Big Dave and Tom gave Liam a thumbs-up from across the street. Liam breathed a sigh of relief. His torment at the hands of Jax and the Darkstone Rangers was over. For now. The game against Darkstone Rangers had become way more than a football match. The bet Tom had made was serious enough. But if Hawk FC lost, Liam must also give up football. Forever.

CHAPTER TWENTY

TOM

Jake's mum drove Tom and Jake to the team's next match, away against St Joseph's FC. It was twenty minutes away from their housing estate, and they arrived at the pitch on a windy day with clouds swirling and empty crisp packets and fallen leaves whipping about the fields. Coach Billy and Jimmy were already there, and most of the team was warming up, so Tom thanked Jake's mum for the lift and ran over to join them.

Jimmy led the team in the same warm-up as Thursday night.

"Call your name!" Jimmy called, reminding each member to call their own name whenever they went up for a pretend header during the warm-up.

Once they had completed the sprints and two

compact rondos, Jimmy brought them together to review the team.

"We'll stick with Coach Billy's team for this week," he explained. He knelt on the grass with a whiteboard in his hands, and the team gathered eagerly around him. "With one slight difference. Liam, you are going to play midfield today and Paulie will start up front. Liam, I want you to play like a number eight. Lots of running. Box to box. Think Steven Gerard or Frank Lampard. Can you do that?"

Liam nodded. "I can do that."

Jimmy turned the whiteboard around to reveal eleven blue, and eleven red magnetic circles stuck to it. He arranged them into two teams and explained how Hawk FC was going to play. Every player listened carefully, leaning in, watching eagerly as Jimmy shifted the magnets around the board to show how to pass out from the back, what to do at corners and how the wingers should play.

"Tom, you're the captain today. Get the lads together and then lead them out," said Jimmy.

Coach Billy tossed a captain's armband to Tom and winked as Tom caught it. Hawk FC had never played with a captain, and the armband was deep black with bright white lettering. It was brand new, and as Tom slipped the armband over his left arm, his heart swelled with pride. Although his kit was faded and frayed, he felt like he was playing in the Premier League. The team was organised. They had a plan, and Tom was their captain.

The referee blew the whistle and St Joseph's took the kick-off. They kicked the ball back to their centre-half, and all their midfielders and their striker charged forward. The centre-half put his foot through the ball and launched it up the field. The ball hung in the air like a soaring bird for what seemed like an age. Tom watched it carefully until he realised it was coming down in his direction. He braced himself, set his feet, and raised his arms level with his chest.

"Tom's ball!" he shouted, and headed the ball right in the middle of his forehead. The ball soared back in the direction it had come from, and Tom glanced to the sideline where Coach Billy and Jimmy both gave him a vigorous thumbs-up. Liam controlled the ball with his right foot and found himself all alone, because the St Joseph's midfielders had all charged forwards. Liam turned quickly and sprinted towards the opponent's goal. He drove straight at the centre-back and when the big lad leapt forward and committed to the tackle, Liam threaded the ball through to Paulie, who whacked it with his left foot. The net bulged and Tom couldn't believe it. Hawk FC was one-nil up in the first minute of the game!

By half-time, Hawk FC was two-nil up and passing the ball around like an actual football team. Just before the whistle blew, Tom had fizzed the ball down the line to Leo and, in the biggest surprise of the day, Leo let the ball run past him and ran after it like a galloping horse. He got his cross in just as the referee blew for the end of the half.

"Are we winning, or am I dreaming?" Big Dave asked as the players gathered on the touchline to grab their bottles of water.

"Not only are we winning, mate," panted Jake, "we are playing well."

"Brilliant, boys," said Jimmy, clapping each player on the back. "Keep it up in the second half."

Tom gulped down some water and returned to the pitch. Every Hawk player took their place before the half was due to begin. They jogged on the spot, eyes wide with excitement, eager to get going again now that they could actually play. The second half kicked off, and Hawk kept pressing St Joseph's hard. Their winger crossed a ball in. It bounced over Jake's head and their striker bundled the ball past Mark in goal. Five minutes later, St Joseph's scored a header from a corner.

Tom and the rest of the Hawks battled to keep the score at two-all, but by the time the match ended, sweat-soaked Tom's hair, and his legs burned fiercely. The team collapsed to the floor and could barely drag themselves to the centre circle to shake hands with the St Joseph's team.

"That's a good start," said Jimmy as he gathered them all together by the clubhouse. "A point won against a good team. We need to work on fitness. There are eight weeks until the next Darkstone game, and we will be ready."

CHAPTER TWENTY-ONE

TOM

Coach Billy and Jimmy worked the team hard. For three weeks, they trained twice per week and they did nothing but run. They ran and ran and at the end of the first week, Tom thought his legs might fall off. Despite the intense training, not one member of the squad missed a session. Hawk FC lost their next game and drew the next one. In week four, Jimmy put them through a test he called the bleep test. The team had to run between two sides of the pitch, turning to run again every time the noise on Jimmy's phone bleeped. Tom could barely breathe by the end, but Jimmy clapped and strode amongst them with his hands on his hips.

"Now we're ready to play football," he had said.

For the next two weeks, Jimmy brought balls back into training. He worked them hard, learning how to transition the ball from defence to midfield and into attack. It was challenging work, but Tom had never seen a group of players so dialled into training. Tom found himself thinking about Jimmy's tactics in bed at night, when he woke up in the morning, and especially when he was daydreaming during maths class.

Hawk FC lined up to play Lewiston FC at home for their next match. Tom had been captain for every match since Coach Billy brought Jimmy on board, and before kick-off, he brought the Hawk FC players into a huddle. They gathered about him, arms around each other's shoulders. Their tarnished kit was frayed and torn, but the players looked lean and hungry.

"We have two more matches before we play Darkstone," Tom said. "Let's go out and win them both. We are fitter now than any other team in the league, and we are much better than we were. Lewiston are mid-table. We can beat these lads. Let's work as a team, be strong, and enjoy it. Are we ready?"

"Yeah!" said the team in unison, nodding at him.

"I said, are we ready?" Liam shouted.

"Ready!" the team yelled back with their eyes blazing.

"On three, then. One, two, three, Hawk FC!" The team roared the last two words as one and ran into their positions, pumping their fists. Ready to play. Ready to win.

The whistle went, and Paulie passed the ball back to Liam. He dribbled around two players and passed the ball out to Leo, who took the ball on his right foot and whipped a cross in. Paulie dived but just missed a header and the ball went out for a goal-kick.

"Good work, Leo!" Tom called across the pitch.

"He's woken up over the last few weeks," commented Jake as they set up for the goal-kick.

"We all have. We have to if we don't want to get relegated, and we certainly don't want to kiss the Darkstone badge."

Tom battled throughout the first half. The Lewiston left-winger was tricky, and every time he got the ball, he dribbled at Tom. Tom tried to remember the defending lessons Jimmy had taught him. Delay the attacker and then get a tackle in when he commits to run past. It worked for most of the first half until the winger jinked past Tom just before half-time. Tom dived in with a badly-timed sliding tackle and the winger was away. He whipped a cross in with his left foot; the ball bounced in the area and their striker poked it past Mark in goal before Jake or Big Dave could get a foot on it. One-nil.

The referee blew for half-time and the Hawk FC players trudged to their coaches with their heads held low. Coach Billy waited for Tom to have a drink and then pulled him to one side.

"You are playing well," Billy said.

"The goal was my fault," Tom sighed. "I'm not good enough, Billy. The winger skinned me."

"You're the captain, Tom. Get your head up and motivate the team to go out and win."

"But how can I do that when we're not strong enough?"

"I believe in you, Tom. I've always believed in you. It's only one-nil. The team needs you now. Come back and win this game and the boys will always remember it. They'll have the knowledge stored away in their minds, that they can fight back from a goal down and win a match. Make them believe." Billy put his hands on either side of Tom's face and stared into his eyes.

Strength surged through Tom's arms and legs. If Billy believed, then Tom believed.

"Come on, boys!" Tom shouted. He went around each player and told them something positive they had done in the first half. He told each of them he believed in them and when the players lined up to begin the second half, they stood with their chests out and their heads held high.

The match re-started, and Lewiston passed the ball around confidently.

"Keep it tight, lads," said one of their midfielders,

a short lad with freckles. "These are rubbish. Let's get three goals this half."

The next thing Tom saw was an enormous shadow surging past him like a storm cloud. The ball rolled into the freckled midfielder's foot and Big Dave came flying in with a crunching slide-tackle. He won the ball cleanly, and the freckled boy crumpled into a heap.

"Come on, Hawk FC!" Big Dave shouted, and Tom felt pride well in his chest, taking hold like a sparking fire.

Liam took the ball on his chest and flicked it over the head of a Lewiston defender. He ran onto the ball, took it around the goalkeeper and smashed the ball into the net. He wheeled away, running with a finger to his lips to hush the cocky Lewiston players, and Tom ran to join in the celebration.

Lewiston fought hard after the equaliser, and the second half was tight. Tom kept the tricky winger at bay whilst Jake and Big Dave both played like Virgil van Dijk at the back. Adam won a vital tackle in midfield and threaded the ball through to Paulie, who raced through on goal only for a Lewiston player to viciously hack him down from behind.

"Ah, ref!" Tom appealed, infuriated at the foul because Paulie would surely have scored.

The referee blew his whistle and pointed to the penalty spot.

"Who's going to take it?" Jake asked, turning to Tom.

"We've never had a penalty before," Tom replied. He turned to Coach Billy.

"You're the captain, Tom," Billy said. "You decide."

Tom felt the weight of pressure on his shoulders. The game stood at one-all, with only a few minutes remaining. If Hawk scored, a win would give them the confidence they so desperately needed. He could take it himself, but Tom was a defender for a reason. Big Dave had a powerful kick on him, but he was wildly inaccurate. Liam. It had to be Liam.

"Liam," Tom stated. He picked up the ball and handed it to Liam. "You take it."

"No, Tom!" Liam shook his head vigorously. "What if I miss?"

"Liam, you've been our best player by a mile since you joined the team. I trust you. Take it, score, and give us the win."

Liam nodded and took a deep breath. He set the ball down, took four steps back, and prepared himself. He glanced at the goal. Liam's feet thundered on the turf in quick steps, and he ran around the ball in a wide arc. He came around the ball and thumped it with his right foot. The net bulged. Top corner. Liam fell to his knees. Hawk FC was two-one up! Tom's heart exploded with joy. He sprinted to Jake, and they jumped around in each other's arms and rushed to Liam to celebrate.

The match kicked off again and after two Lewiston passes, the referee blew for full-time. Hawk FC had won! Not only had they won, but they had played well, and Tom punched his fist into the air.

CHAPTER TWENTY-TWO

LIAM

Liam smiled for two days straight after beating Lewiston FC.

"You seem happy," said Mum as she dropped him off at training on Tuesday night.

"Yeah, I suppose I am," he replied with a shrug.

"Do you like it here now, then?"

"I like the team. School is getting better, I suppose."

"Do you still miss Ronan and your friends?"

Liam realised he hadn't thought about Ronan or Park Celtic for a week. He still missed his best friend and his teammates, but not with the crippling sadness of his first weeks in England. "I miss them. But I'm OK, Mum."

"Well, it's lovely to see you smiling."

Liam leaned over the seat and planted a kiss on her cheek, and Mum smiled like it was Christmas. He got out of the car and hurried over to the Hawk's Nest, where the lads were about to start their warm-up with Jimmy and Coach Billy. Jimmy brought them through a series of technical passing drills inside a square cornered by cones.

"I can't believe we can actually pass the ball like this," marvelled Mark as the ball pinged around the players, each pass quick and flat to the grass.

"It's brilliant," Liam grinned.

"Tom, Liam!" Jimmy waved the two boys over.

"What's up, Jimmy?" asked Liam as they both jogged over to where the coach waited for them by the goal.

"I want to show you something. A special move that might just help in your big game against Darkstone."

"OK, great," said Tom.

"This is something I used to do with Liverpool reserves. You can only do it once per game. It will only work once because the opposition will look for it once you've done it. So, save it until you really need it."

Jimmy walked them through the special move he called a right full-back overlap. When Liam won the ball in midfield, he was to pass the ball back to Tom and come towards the right-wing. Tom was to pass the ball back into him and run an overlap down the wing around the right-winger. Liam would fizz the ball down towards the corner flag, and Tom would cross it in first time for Liam to finish on the volley.

"It's a complicated one," Jimmy said after they had been through it five times. "But if you get it right, the other team won't be able to defend it."

Liam looked at Tom and they both nodded at Jimmy. Liam had scored two out of the five practice runs. It depended on Tom's cross, and Liam connecting with the ball on the volley. It was a risk, but Liam could see how it would cut through an opponent's defence like a hot knife through butter.

The session went well, and they finished with a match at the end, where Tom scored the winner for Liam's team with a bullet header.

"Everybody gather around before you go," called Coach Billy at the end of training. The team laughed and joked around, with Tom and Jake wrestling each other, and Mark and Big Dave squirting each other with their water bottles.

"OK, lads, everybody in," said Jimmy, and the squad gathered around. "I've really enjoyed working with you guys over the last few weeks. We've got you to a strong level of fitness and thoroughly improved your basic skills. You have everything you need to go on and win the game against Darkstone. Unfortunately, my time here is over. I've got a new job working with Bolton Wanderers, so I won't be able to work with you anymore. Billy knows what he's doing and is committed to helping you all continue to improve."

"Well done, Jimmy," beamed Coach Billy.

Liam's mouth fell open and his stomach lurched. Just as the team was improving, and a week before the Darkstone game, Jimmy was leaving!

"Don't leave us, Jimmy," wailed Leo, saying what every player was thinking.

"I have to work, lads," Jimmy spoke gently. "You don't need me anymore. You have everything you need to beat Darkstone."

"We're just disappointed, Jimmy, that's all," said Tom. "But we all thank you for everything you have done for us."

Liam couldn't believe it. It was just like leaving Ireland. When everything was going well for him, something came out of the blue to knock him down. How could they win without Jimmy? If Hawk FC lost, Liam would have to give up football. Forever. He walked to Mum's car feeling numb, wondering if things could get any worse.

CHAPTER TWENTY-THREE

TOM

Match day came around quickly and Tom travelled to the Darkstone Rangers' ground in Jake's car. They remained silent for the entire journey. Tom stared out of the window, unable to think of anything but how bad it would be if they lost. Nothing else mattered but winning. The Darkstone Rangers' ground was everything the Hawk's Nest wasn't. Sponsorship signs lined the road leading into the ground, including one with a snarling bulldog. The Darkstone Rangers' black and white painted clubhouse in pristine condition loomed like a thundercloud as they drove into the car park. White flag posts ran the length of the car park and black flags whipped and cracked in the wind.

Tom and Jake thanked Jake's mum for the lift and walked to the away changing room, still silent and full of fear.

"Chicken FC," leered Jax, leaning against the outside of the clubhouse. "I hope you haven't forgotten about our bet."

"We haven't forgotten," snapped Tom, but he wished he had never made it.

"Remember, losers, if we win, you'll forfeit the rest of your matches and be relegated. And you have to line up after the game and kiss our badge."

Tom's anger flared. He was sick of the Darkstone players thinking they were better than Hawk FC. "When we win, you clean our boots here while we watch, and you take our kit and wash it!"

"I can't wait to see you lose. Where's that Irish muppet of yours?"

"Just leave him alone, Jax."

"I have left him alone, just like we agreed. But today is the day where he suffers."

Tom took a step towards Jax, but Jake grabbed him by the arm and pulled him away.

"We'll settle this on the pitch," Jake said, and Tom let his friend lead him away as Jax laughed at them.

Tom entered the changing room to find the rest of the team waiting for him. They sat with their heads bowed, and the room was as quiet as a library.

"Come on lads," Tom said brightly. "Let's get our

heads up!"

"Why?" asked Mark. "Jimmy's gone. Sergio is still injured. We're about to get humiliated."

Liam walked in and sat down on the changing room benches. His face was as white as a ghost.

"Are you all right, Liam?" Tom asked.

Liam looked at him, and for a moment, Tom thought he might cry. "I just bumped into Jax outside."

"He's a bully. You are twice the player he is. Ignore him."

"When I asked the Darkstone lads to leave me alone at school, they only agreed because I promised Jax that if we lose, I'll never play football again."

"Well, we'd better win, then," said Coach Billy as he bustled into the changing room. "You lads making these silly bets with a team at the top of the league." Billy tutted and shook his head. He dropped a large blue kit bag down in the centre of the changing room floor. "Jimmy called around to see me this morning. He's sorry he can't be here but has a present for us."

Tom stared at the bag. "What is it, Billy?"

"Open it up and see."

Tom unzipped the bag and stared inside, and it was as though pure gold gleamed back at him.

He reached in and pulled out a brand-new number ten jersey. It was gold, with a picture of a hawk with outstretched wings across the bottom half and green stripes down the arms.

"It's amazing," Tom whispered as if he had just uncovered a piece of ancient treasure.

"There's more," beamed Billy.

Tom dug deeper into the bag and found a pair of green shorts and green and gold striped socks for every player on the team.

"Jimmy says he got the kit because you boys deserve it," Billy explained. "He says you can play like a wonderful team, so you should also look like one. Now. Get your kit on, get out there and beat Darkstone Rangers!"

Tom pulled on his kit and instantly felt a foot taller. *We can do this,* he thought, and they had to— because to lose was unthinkable.

CHAPTER TWENTY-FOUR

LIAM

Liam took his place on the pitch, wearing his new kit and feeling like a footballer. The smell of recently cut grass filled his nose and the corner flags snapped and blew in the breeze.

Darkstone made their huddle, broke, and moved into a single-line formation, like soldiers standing to attention.

"Crush them! Hurt them! Beat them! Own them!" the Darkstone players roared in perfect unison. In their all-black kit, they made a fearsome spectacle, their faces focused and stern, sending a shiver of fear across Liam's shoulders.

"I'm coming for you, muppet," Jax shouted across the centre circle, but Liam ignored him.

This was football. Not like at school, where Jax had his friends to protect him. This was Darkstone Rangers against Hawk Football Club, and in his new kit, with the soft grass crunching beneath his boots, Liam felt the fresh breeze blow all his fears away.

Jax lined up at centre-back beside Buzz Cut, the stocky boy who had allowed Liam to escape when they had cut his tie and laces at school.

"We can do this, lads!" Tom called from right-back, and Liam hoped he was right.

The game kicked off and Darkstone passed the ball back to their midfielders. Liam ran forward and tried to make a tackle, but they passed around him with quick, accurate passes. They chipped a ball forward and Jake headed it away. Liam darted to the ball, but a Darkstone midfielder crashed into him and barged him out of the way. He chased after the ball, but everywhere he went, Liam was too late. He was second to every ball, too late for every interception, and Big Dave made a last-ditch tackle as the Darkstone striker was through on goal.

Hawk FC was just about hanging onto nil-nil, but Liam hadn't touched the ball yet.

"Liam!" Tom shouted. "Get your head in the game. We need you!"

Liam took a breath. *You can do it*, he told himself. *You have to do it. It's now or never!*

The ball broke from a throw-in and Liam controlled it on his knee. It dropped to his right foot, and he passed it down the line for Leo, who ran after it, but the ball went out of touch.

"My granny's got a better touch than you!" crowed Jax. It stung, but Liam said nothing. He moved up the pitch for the Darkstone throw-in. It came in and Big Dave won the header, barging a Darkstone player to the floor. Liam took the ball on his left foot and threaded it through to Paulie, who set off sprinting past Jax towards the goal.

"Go on, Paulie!" Mark cheered.

Paulie took a touch and reached the edge of the area, but Jax slid right through him from behind and Paulie screamed in pain. The referee ran towards Paulie and flashed a yellow card at Jax.

"You're next, muppet," Jax threatened, pointing at Liam.

Coach Billy came running onto the pitch and helped Paulie limp off. Paulie shook his head, tears streaming down his face, unable to continue playing. Hawk FC was down to ten men with no substitutes. Jax had put a disgraceful tackle in, and Paulie's match was over. Adam took the free kick, but his shot sailed over the bar. The next ten minutes were a battle as Darkstone passed it around well, but Hawk FC kept them away from the goal.

Tom picked the ball up at right-back and passed

it to Liam. He took it on the half-turn, danced around a Darkstone midfielder and ran at Jax. Jax came at him charging like a bull, just as Liam knew he would. Liam stepped over the ball with his left foot and Jax bought the dummy. He shifted the ball with his right foot and was away, leaving Jax staring after him. Liam took two more touches, aware of the other centre-back chasing after him. The Darkstone goalkeeper came out and Liam scooped the ball over him with a deft chip. Liam wheeled away as the ball bounced on the line and went into the goal to put Hawk FC one-nil up.

"What a goal!" screamed Big Dave and the entire Hawk FC team descended on Liam, cheering and clapping him on the back.

Liam couldn't believe it. He had scored and Hawk FC was in the lead! Darkstone got together in a huddle and came to the centre circle with fiercely determined looks on their faces.

"No mercy!" their horrible coach barked from the sideline. "Take them out! Destroy them!"

The Darkstone striker kicked off the game and passed the ball back to their midfielder, who made a lazy pass which rolled into Liam's feet. He controlled the ball, surprised at the mistake.

"Liam!" Tom cried out behind him. "Look out!"

Liam looked up just in time to see Jax hurtling towards him like a train. The pass hadn't been a mistake. It was a set-up. Before Liam could get out of the way, Jax crunched into him with two feet. His studs raked Liam's ankle, and it felt like a knife cutting through his bones and ligaments. Liam fell to the grass, clutching his ankle and roaring with pain.

Coach Billy came running onto the pitch and helped Liam to his feet. The Darkstone and Hawk players shouted at each other in outrage, and the referee's whistle blew repeatedly as he tried to bring the match under control.

"Can you put any weight on it?" Billy asked.

Liam tried to put his injured foot down, but it burned like fire. "I can't, Billy, he's done me."

Billy helped Liam limp from the pitch and slumped down next to Paulie on the sideline. Hawk FC was down to nine men, and Jax didn't even get a second yellow card for his foul on Liam. Within thirty seconds, Jax scored a header from a corner and pointed to Liam as he celebrated. Darkstone scored again before half-time and Liam felt hollow inside. Hawk FC was losing, and this could be his last ever game of football.

CHAPTER TWENTY-FIVE

TOM

The whistle went for half-time and the Darkstone Rangers cheered like they had already won the match. Tom stalked from the pitch with the sound of their celebrations ringing in his ears.

"What are we going to do?" moaned Jake, running his hands through his sweat-soaked hair. "We're down to nine men. They are tearing us apart!"

"We have to find a way," murmured Tom. He couldn't admit it out loud, but it looked like Hawk FC was done for.

Tom grabbed his water bottle and sat down on the grass. The team gathered about him, exchanging nervous looks, unable to utter any words of encouragement to each other.

"It's only two-one, lads," Coach Billy encouraged

them. "You've all played brilliantly."

"We might as well give up now," muttered Mark, and he pulled off his goalie gloves and hurled them to the ground.

"We have to carry on," Tom stated, feeling the need to say something positive even though he didn't feel it.

"All right, boys?" came a chirpy voice. One Tom hadn't heard for a long time. "Sorry, I'm late. My dad thought the match was at the Nest, so we went there first."

"Sergio?" gasped Big Dave, rising to his feet, mouth gaping in surprise.

"Yeah, I'm fit again," grinned Sergio. "Nice kit! Is there a jersey for me in the bag?"

"Billy," said Tom, rising to his feet, heart thumping in his chest. "Give Sergio a jersey. Lads, we've got our star striker back!" Tom couldn't remember how many times Sergio had scored goals out of nothing. In most seasons, he was the difference between them and relegation.

"We're back to ten men!" whooped Jake.

"Billy?" asked Liam, lying on the ground, holding his ankle. "Is there any tape in the kit bag?"

"There is. Lots of it," Billy replied after he tossed Sergio a number twelve jersey.

"Tape up my ankle then. Wrap it tight so it can't move."

"Wait," said Tom. "Are you going to play?"

"It's either that, or never play again. You lads were kind to me when I had no friends. Hawk FC gave me something to believe in when I moved to England and felt all alone. I owe you guys everything. We are Hawk FC, and we can beat these bullies."

Billy wrapped Liam's ankle until he could limp about. Liam gritted his teeth and hobbled up and down the touchline until the limp turned into a run. Tom looked around at each of his teammates, and he saw the fire of belief burning behind their eyes.

We can do this!

The second half kicked off and Sergio passed the ball back to Liam. Liam controlled it and passed it back to Jake, who booted the ball upfield. Leo challenged the Darkstone full-back, but the ball went out of play. This was it. Hawk FC had one half of football to defeat their greatest enemies. The ball whipped around the pitch, with quick passes, hard tackles, and fair shoulders. Most of the second half was like a pinball machine. Tom won three tackles and cheered each one like he had scored a goal. Jake and Big Dave kept the Darkstone strikers at bay, and Liam kept things moving in midfield.

The Darkstone full-back hefted a long ball into the Hawk FC box, and the dangerous situation forced

Jake to head it out for a corner.

"Let's crush these worms," snarled Jax as both teams jostled each other, waiting for the ball to come in.

"You've injured two of our players," said Big Dave, staring at Jax with a thunderous look on his face.

"They were wimps. Just like you, Little Dave." Jax turned to his teammates, and they laughed at his joke. Just like they always did.

Dave took up a position on the near-post and Jax waited on the penalty spot. Tom marked him, pushing Jax with his shoulder, and Jax shoved him back. The cross came in, high and looping, towards the centre of the box. Big Dave grunted and charged out, leaping in the air and hammering into Jax like a charging elephant. He headed the ball away and Jax fell to the grass, whimpering like a kitten.

The ball broke to Liam. He spun like a dancer and ran up the pitch. Sergio made a darting run beyond the one defender Darkstone had left back during the corner. Liam chipped the ball over that player and Sergio took the ball in his stride. He ran, using his speed to get away from the defender, and as he reached the edge of the box, he unleashed a mighty shot with his left foot. The ball flew like an arrow and hit the back of the Darkstone net so hard Tom thought it might burst through.

The Hawk FC players went crazy, leaping about

the pitch to congratulate Sergio. Tom turned from the celebrations just in time to see Big Dave towering over Jax, who still lay crying on the grass. Tom couldn't hear what Dave said to Jax, but it wasn't pretty by the look on his face. It was two-all. A draw. But Hawk FC was back in it!

The game kicked off again and Darkstone threw everything they had at Hawk FC. Tom put in more tackles than he could remember making in one match before and his teammates fought like lions to keep Darkstone away from the goal. The game went on, the ball hurtling from one end of the pitch to the other.

"How long's left, ref?" Mark shouted.

"One minute," the ref called back.

The ball went out for a goal kick to Hawk FC and Tom waved to Liam.

"Liam?" he shouted, and the Irish midfielder looked at him, his face drenched with sweat and his ankle heavy with tape. "Let's do Jimmy's trick!"

It was time. Time to win this thing.

CHAPTER TWENTY-SIX

LIAM

Liam readied himself, going through Jimmy's move in his mind. Their brilliant coach had left to take a new job, but he had left something with which Liam could defeat his bullies once and for all. Mark, the goalie, passed the ball to Tom, and Tom ran forward. Liam came out to the right flank and Tom fizzed a great pass into Liam's foot.

"Overlap," Tom shouted.

Liam gritted his teeth and controlled the ball, pain shooting through his injured ankle like a thousand nails were stuck into his skin. He turned on the ball and held off a Darkstone midfielder with his arm. With his uninjured foot, he drilled the ball down the line towards the corner flag where Tom was already sprinting. Liam set off, forcing himself to ignore the pain in his ankle, and sprinted through the Darkstone players. Jax shouted something, but

Liam ignored him. He ran into the box just as Tom reached the ball. Tom wrapped his right foot around it and crossed it in.

Liam set himself adjusting his position, pain tearing at his ankle. He jumped, reading the flight of the ball. It was arriving behind him. Liam had run slightly too far. So, he turned in the air, shaping for a bicycle kick and the ball came down perfectly. Everything around Liam went quiet. This was it. His chance to win the match! He turned at the hip and was about to thump the ball with his right foot when something big and heavy crashed into him, sending Liam tumbling to the ground.

The ball bounced harmlessly next to him, and every player on the Hawk FC team threw their hands up and shouted at the referee.

"Got you again," taunted Jax, leaning over Liam with an angry look on his face.

"Penalty!" the referee screeched. He blew his whistle and pointed to the spot. "That was a terrible challenge! You are off!" He pulled a red card from his pocket and showed it to Jax, who stormed off the pitch, throwing his hands in the air like a baby who had lost its dummy.

"It's yours, Liam," panted Tom, reaching down to help Liam to his feet. "This is the last kick of the game. We all believe in you. Do it for the boys. Do it for Hawk FC."

Liam nodded, stood, dusted himself down and picked up the ball.

"Go for it, Liam!" yelled Big Dave.

Liam took a breath and set the ball down on the penalty spot. The light breeze blew across the pitch and cooled the sweat on his brow. He took only one step back, not trusting his injured ankle for a run-up. The Darkstone goalie jumped up and down on the line, trying to put Liam off, but he ignored him. It was all in Liam's hands. An end to the bullying. Hawk would stay in the league, and Darkstone would be humiliated.

The whistle went. Liam took one step forward. He paused mid-stride, and the goalkeeper bought the feint, lurching to his left. That was all Liam needed. He passed the ball into the opposite corner, and it rolled into the back of the net.

Liam fell to his knees, feelings of relief and triumph washing over him like a tidal wave. His teammates dived on him, going crazy with joy and somewhere, amongst the chaos of victory, Liam heard the referee blow for full-time. Liam stood, limping on his bad ankle as the Hawk FC players ran towards Coach Billy. An arm reached around his back, and somebody was helping him to walk.

It was Buzz Cut. "You played well today, mate," the Darkstone player said with a smile. "Fair play. I'm sorry about all the trouble with Jax. I'll make sure he doesn't bother you again."

"Thanks," Liam replied, surprised to see one of his enemies helping him. "You played well yourself."

"I guess I'm going to be washing your boots, then?"

"Looks like it."

"That was a brilliant move at the end. I thought you were going to nail that bicycle kick!"

Liam smiled. He loved playing for Hawk Football Club, and he loved football.

Don't you?

A NOTE FROM
THE AUTHOR

Thanks for reading Hawk Football Club. I hope you enjoyed the story and that you're excited for more books about the team.

I would like to thank a few special editors and co-writers – Sean, Rian and Liadh. They are my children who read and contributed to the first draft, and made the story what it is. I wrote this book to feed their hunger and passion for football, a topic they can never read too much about.

As a football coach and father I wanted to write this book to entertain and encourage all children with a love for football. The core themes are friendship, sportsmanship, dedication and enjoyment of the game. I hope every child who reads the book comes away hungry for more football...

ABOUT THE AUTHOR

Stevie Suarez

Stevie Suarez is the pen name of best-selling historical fiction author Peter Gibbons.

Born and raised in Warrington in the North West of England, Peter wanted to be an author from the age of ten when he first began to write stories.

Since then, Peter has written many books, including the bestselling Viking Blood and Blade Saga, the Saxon Warrior Series, and the Chronicles of Arthur.

Peter was the winner of the Kindle Storyteller Literary award in 2022, he lives in Kildare, Ireland with his wife and three children.

Printed in Great Britain
by Amazon